GOD'S ANTIDOTE FOR DEPRESSION, ANXIETY, OR FEAR

LEARN HOW TO EXPERIENCE PEACE AND JOY DURING ADVERSITY AND UNCERTAIN TIMES

God's Antidote for Depression, Anxiety, or Fear

Learn How to Experience Peace and Joy During Adversity and Uncertain Times

Debby Sibert

A Note from the Author:

It is my heart's desire that everyone would have an opportunity to meet Jesus – to experience Him intimately, to have their hearts transformed by His love and grace, and to learn the peace, joy, and victory that comes from a "sold-out" life of surrender and obedience. Do you know Him?

Running theme of this book is found in Philippians 4

Key verses:

4:11, *"Not that I am speaking of being in need, for I have learned in whatever situation I am to be content."*

4:13, *"I can do all things through Him who strengthens me."*

4:19, *"And my God will supply every need of yours according to his riches in glory in Christ Jesus"*

DISCLAIMER:

As I state in this book, I am not a doctor, counselor, or therapist. I am not a psychologist, or psychiatrist. I am coming at these topics from a pastoral perspective to give a message of hope as to how God can help us navigate difficult times.

In no way, do I try to address *clinical* depression, anxiety, or mental illness, as that would be above my pay grade. In no way do I propose to offer a medical cure for anything. Sometimes professional, medical help is necessary for anxiety, depression and mental illness, and I don't want the reader in any way to think that I am ignoring or minimizing that reality. If that is you and you haven't already, please get help and realize that there is no shame in seeking help from a medical professional or counselor.

I have studied these issues enough to know that most people struggling with depression, anxiety or fear do not fall in the "clinical" category. If you do, and are getting the proper treatment, this book can be beneficial even for you.

These are complex emotions and volumes could be written on each. This booklet is intended to be a cursory overview of each with examples of how putting our trust and faith in the faithful God who created us, we can experience peace and joy during adversity and uncertain times. This book was written to give hope to the hopeless, which only God can do. He is faithful and true. We can trust His promises.

ACKNOWLEDGEMENTS

To my wonderful husband, who has sacrificed many days and nights of solitude while I worked tirelessly on this manuscript. Thank you also for your prayers, proofreading, editing, and valuable feedback along the way. God has used you mightily to help me become the wife, mother, friend, and Christ-follower I am today. You inspire me with your life of honesty, integrity, and servant leadership, as well as your love and devotion. This just scratches the surface of your many qualities I hope have rubbed off on me over these forty years of sharing life. You are my rock. Thank you for believing in me and supporting me to fulfill God's purpose in getting this book out of my head and heart and into print.

To my pastor of almost thirty years, Lon Solomon, who unknowingly consistently mentored me from the pulpit, inspiring me to speak the truth about the gospel boldly, I thank you. My current pastor, David Platt, I thank you for the continuing challenge to deepen my faith and live it out daily with a mission mindset. Both of you have significantly contributed to my understanding of the importance of total surrender and obedience.

In addition to my pastors I have had the privilege of hearing in person on Sundays, I have been blessed to find the Chip Ingram app which I have on my phone and listen to pretty much every weekday as I take my morning walks. This is a pastor who loves God and the Scriptures and teaches with great passion what he understands from God's Word. He is a great communicator. Besides what I have learned from the Scriptures themselves and my own personal experience, most of the information I gathered for this book has been absorbed into my life over a couple years of listening to these podcasts. He also has a website, likewise full of great resources: https://livingontheedge.org.

I want to give him credit and a "shout-out" because he and his messages truly have encouraged me and been instrumental to the maturity of my faith and inspired me to apply what I have learned, especially in preparation for writing this book.

He has repurpose his sermons and turned them into daily podcasts that are life-changing. I cannot recommend this app enough. It is free as well as all the messages, and are available for any device. Check out the "Chip Ingram" app.

Most of all, I want to thank my Lord and Savior, Jesus Christ, who is always with me to help me get through anything. I know Him to be sovereign, in control, full of love, grace, mercy, and forgiveness, always looking out for my best interests.

He is faithful to His Word and His promises, for which I am truly grateful. While I occasionally experience some adversity and uncertainties, I know I can count on Him to give me that inner strength and incomprehensible peace and joy to get me through it. I pray you will read this to the end, so you too can learn to experience that inner peace that is possible when you know where to go and what to do.

TABLE OF CONTENTS

In memory of my dear friend, Bethi Wyatt
who lost her battle with depression this year.
May the lessons we learned from her experience help
bring hope to those who feel the hopelessness that she felt.

INTRODUCTION

At the time of this writing, our world is experiencing a global crisis—a worldwide pandemic of a new coronavirus (COVID-19). There is no cure, and any hope for a vaccine is in the distant future. At the time of this writing, there have been many millions of cases globally, including over eight million cases in the United States alone, and over 200,000 deaths, also in the US. Those numbers continue to climb. Travel has been restricted, and people have been ordered to stay home unless they have to go out for medical reasons, groceries, or to work.

Most people, if they can, work from home. If we go anywhere, we are expected to wear a face mask and keep a physical distance of at least six feet. Many commodities we usually take for granted have become scarce. Schools and businesses have shut down. Unemployment has hit an all-time high, and the stock market has tanked. We are told this is far from over, and we could easily have a reoccurrence as restrictions are lifted. This is unnerving since people need to go back to work. The economy is in a recession.

Our world *has* experienced some times worse than this, but not in our lifetime. If we ever lived in an uncertain time with an unclear future and reason to fear, it is now. We need to watch enough news to be informed and know how we need to respond based on public health experts' advice, but this situation is enough to cause even the most stable individual to have significant concerns. Fear is a natural response for humans and has its place to help keep us safe. However, living in fear is counter-productive and is not an option if we will get through this or any other difficult circumstance. We cannot allow ourselves to get stuck there and dwell on these negative issues.

Individuals experience adversity manifested by fear, anxiety, and even depression for many reasons, and our world seems to be growing more and more fearful every day. The news media is adept at covering the goriest of details that bring violent crimes into our homes, feeding the trough of human despair. Suicides have become commonplace, especially among the youth, while disease, accidents, death, and corruption personify our broken, fallen world.

This is far from an exhaustive discourse the subject, but my goal and message in this short book, is to offer hope to the broken and downhearted — the depressed, anxious or fearful. I define these emotional states, discussing the symptoms and some causes for each, and how to overcome them biblically. One cannot read this book without being changed from the inside out if the shared truths are taken seriously, acted upon, and allowed to permeate and become a reality in your heart and mind.

I have learned God's antidote to the fear and uncertainty that often leads to anxiety and depression. I want more than anything to share it with you because I am confident you can find relief for your souls through the message I believe the Lord has given me to share with you, using His Word as our guide.

CHAPTER 1

WHAT IS ADVERSITY?

I would say that depression, anxiety, and fear all fall under the umbrella of adversity, so let's take a look at that first. Dictonary.com defines adversity as a condition marked by misfortune, calamity, or distress. What seems difficult or challenging to one person may seem insignificant to another, so there is a wide range of what can be considered adversity. No question, we all will experience it in varying degrees in our lifetime. You have picked up this book because you probably are experiencing some adversity right now, looking for answers or relief.

Have you ever gotten to the point where you feel like you can never rise above your circumstances? Do you ever feel like life is too hard? Do you ever tell yourself, "I'm done? I've had it? I can't take it anymore? I'm opting out?"

This is a very dark place to be. As you read through all the things I'm going to suggest to you, your response might be, "I've already heard all of that, and none of it works for me. You don't know what all I've been through. You don't know how badly I've been hurt." Maybe you've even gone so far in your mind that you entertain fantasies of how to dull or mute the pain, and you have begun to drift.

May I encourage you to hear me out, think back to good times in your life, and focus on the positive rather than the darkness you may now be experiencing. No, this is not just a "feel good—positive thinking" type of book. My goal is to lift you out of this state and not only bring you to a much better place, but also to an extraordinary state of peace, joy and contentment you never thought possible.

I am not a psychologist or psychiatrist with advanced degrees, so I am not giving medical advice nor calling my message a "medical cure." No way am I trying to offer a simple Band-Aid of spiritual sounding rhetoric to someone suffering the paralyzing effects of fear, panic, anxiety, or depression.

What I am offering with biblical truth is not a substitution for medication or therapy for those who need it, but rather something that can complement and supplement that for those looking for a breakthrough.

I will not be addressing clinical depression or mental illness because that is far above my pay grade. But because I know the Creator of all things who gives generously to those who ask, I will share the wisdom of the God of the universe, based on His Word, the Scriptures, which if taken to heart and acted upon, will change your life, not only for now, but also for eternity.

Your experience and pain is not unique. You need to know that. You are actually in good company. Sir Winston Churchill, President Abraham Lincoln, and actor Robin Williams are just a few famous people who suffered from depression. Churchill called it, "The Black Dog." Depression is prevalent and lacks discrimination in whomever it affects.

Many have gone before you who have done terrible things—not saying you have or that is the reason for your current internal struggle. But there *are* many people, even in the Bible, who messed up their lives and had good reason to be depressed because of their personal failure. However, because of their faith in the God of forgiveness, they pushed through the pain, and the struggle of restoration, and ended up in the "Hall of Faith" listed in Hebrews 11 in the New Testament. Why? Because of their willingness to hang in there and endure the hardship with the knowledge of God's promises to get them through it. There is great reward for those willing to press ahead no matter what—yes, even through the pain.

You may be saying to yourself, "I can't do this." You are right. There is no way in your efforts that you can. That is why you need to read what follows carefully because there is a message for you somewhere in these pages. Someone once said, "I can't. God never said I could. He can. He always said He would." If you don't have a relationship with your Creator, you need to realize He is your only hope for true peace and joy in this very troubled world in which we live.

> *"I can't. God never said I could. He can. He always said He would."*

King David, who suffered so much in the Old Testament—some circumstantial, some self-inflicted, and some as a spiritual battle, declares in Psalm 34:17-19 "When the righteous cry for help, the LORD hears and delivers them out of all their troubles. The LORD is near to the brokenhearted and saves the crushed in spirit. Many are the afflictions of the righteous, but the LORD delivers him out of them all."

If you are a Christ-follower, you have learned even though you are considered righteous in God's sight, you will still have suffering. God didn't spare His own Son from suffering, so why would we think He would spare us? We certainly may have many afflictions, but we can rest in the assurance that the "Lord of All" will get us through it if we give it to Him, Can I get an "Amen?"

You need to believe that God wants to help you. First, before we can get any help, we need to admit our need. He knows full well what is going on and could bail you out at any time, but most of all, He wants to wean you from your self-sufficiency and pride. I hope you never hit rock bottom, but if you do, the only way to look is up, isn't it? Until we come to the end of ourselves, we are just playing games. When we admit that we are powerless in our situation, He is near to the brokenhearted and broken in spirit as it says above from Psalm 34, and He offers deliverance.

If you look carefully at these verses, it does not say that David whispered a simple, unemotional rote prayer. He *"cried out"* to the Lord. Our prayers need to be those of total abandon, filled with emotional need and surrender. We know that Jesus often went away to pray, but we probably just think of Him as silently talking to His Father, getting His marching orders for the day. But remember His prayer in the garden of Gethsemane when He knew He was about to be arrested and crucified?

Hebrews 5: 7-8 tells us, "In the days of his flesh, Jesus offered up prayers and supplications, with *loud cries and tears*, to him who was able to save him from death, and he was heard because of his reverence. Although he was a son, he learned obedience through what he suffered." Remember that besides being

I hope you never hit rock bottom, but if you do, the only way to look is up, isn't it?

fully God in the flesh, Jesus also was fully man. He experienced temptation and physical and emotional pain, just like we do. He dreaded like you and I would, the humiliation, the physical suffering of the worst kind of death possible, and the imminent wrath of God separating them as He took upon Himself all the sins of humanity for all time.

This prayer in the garden was not a simple prayer of obedience, although the Bible says in verse 8 that He learned obedience as a human would through what He suffered. He cried out with loud cries. He even asked if there was a plan B that might save Him from having to go through with plan A. However, He knew and always carried out the Father's will. This was no exception as He submitted to the will of the Father regarding the manner of His upcoming death.

He knew why He came, and so for salvation to be accomplished, He had to surrender to His Father' will, which He willingly did. In Luke 22, the author graphically describes Jesus as being so destressed and distraught over this, that His sweat became as drops of blood. We have since learned that is an actual condition called hematidrosis, which is the effusion of blood in

11

one's perspiration which can be caused by extreme anguish or physical strain. Subcutaneous capillaries dilate and burst, mingling blood with sweat.

Jesus had stated that His distress had brought Him to the threshold of death in Mark 14. I'm sure He was tempted to opt-out, but He didn't. He modeled for us the greatest prayer of submission, "Nevertheless, not my will but yours be done" (Luke 22:42).

Paul encourages us in Romans 5:3-5 where he says, "We rejoice in our sufferings, knowing that suffering produces endurance, and endurance produces character, and character produces hope, and hope does not put us to shame, because God's love has been poured into our hearts through the Holy Spirit who has been given to us." The "hope" spoken of here is not at "hope so" hope, but a "know so" hope. It is an assurance of what is to come.

> *He modeled for us the greatest prayer of submission, "Nevertheless, not my will but yours be done." (Luke 22:42)*

It's essential to find the source or root of your adversity; otherwise, chances are, your response will hinder rather than help you grow through it. The best person to help you with that is the Holy Spirit.

Wise, godly people can be helpful, but real "permanent" change will only occur when you find solace in the Scriptures. Only the Word of God will give you His wisdom, guidance, and the strength to persevere.

We must remember that nothing is impossible with God. Have you ever thought that good could come out of adversity? Is it possible that what you are experiencing could be for your good in the long run? Os Hillman, author and speaker who experienced adversity on many levels, would tell you "Yes." He said, "Adversity changes us. Adversity is the crucible that melts down the old us. Adversity is the hammer that shapes the new us."

If we are just concentrating on how to get through our adversity or how to avoid it, we miss out on life. Author Neale Donald Walsch once said, "Life begins at the end of your comfort zone." Adversity is normal, it should be expected, and it can be very powerful. God wants to transform our life through adversity. If you look at some of the most influential individuals you know who stand out with confidence, charisma, whatever you think is admirable, no doubt they have emerged from much suffering. I'm sure there are people in your life that you esteem. They are those who did not opt-out or give up when times got hard. They trusted God. There are difficult things we must suffer through at every stage of our life.

> *"Adversity changes us. Adversity is the crucible that melts down the old us. Adversity is the hammer that shapes the new us."*

Granted, some individuals have more stamina than others; and some seem to have been given more than their share of burdens. No matter what life throws at you, God wants to use it to grow you in your walk with Him to confirm, strengthen, and establish you.

We have a tendency just to live for the now, but we need to live in the now in light of eternity. That's how people can live with an inner joy, even during unhappiness and difficult circumstances. That sounds like an oxymoron, doesn't it? It's true. It is possible to have joy amid the storms of life. I call that being content despite our circumstances and will expand on that later.

When we endure, we expect adversity to be normal, and look to Scripture to encourage us. When we do, we will notice our attitude, outlook, and demeanor start to change. We will find ourselves becoming much more positive instead of focusing on what's lacking.

When we look at adversity biblically, we see it as an uninvited, unwanted guest in the hands of an all-knowing God. Adversity is not our enemy. We can come to this conclusion when we choose to trust God in all things. If you were to look in the rearview mirror of your life, you could probably see times when you thought adversity struck, but as you reflect on it, you can be grateful that things did *not* work out the way you had hoped they would at the time. God wants what's best for us, and that is not always what we think we want. We have such limited vision as to what is best for us. So often we are wrong, but God knows our future and what's best for us, and he *wants* that for us.

> *"Life begins at the end of your comfort zone."*

I will be unpacking this later, but the timeless truth we must glean from this and the theme of this book is, "I can do all things through Him to gives me strength" (Philippians 4:13).

CHAPTER 2

WHAT IS DISCOURAGEMENT?

We spend so much of our time trying to avoid adversity, don't we? No question, it isn't easy. Why is it so important to persevere? Believe it or not, as much as we hate it, the greatest achievements, relationships, discoveries, positive impact, the times of greatest growth, the greatest things that will ever happen during your journey on this earth will either be birthed through adversity or it will be forged and shaped during a difficult time. Most people who get overwhelmed, discouraged and quit, do so just before they would have had a breakthrough.

There are many examples I could cite, but to pick a few—what If Thomas Edison had given up after his 999th failure with the light bulb? He had over 1000 failures before he experienced success. What if Elvis had listened to the stage manager when he had the opportunity to make his debut at the Grand ole' Opry and the stage manager told him he should go back to driving trucks because he would never make it as a singer. Then there's Michael Jordan, who was cut from his high school basketball team. What if he settled for the notion he was no good?

What are you going through right now where God is telling you *not* to bail? He has a purpose in it, but it is easy to get overwhelmed and discouraged. The enemy's greatest tool is discouragement. Don't let him win that struggle!

God has at least three purposes for adversity:

1. To wean us from our self-dependency and pride
2. To usher us into a deeper intimacy with Christ
3. To redirect our paths for our greater good and His glory

The strength, capacity, and confidence that grows from overcoming afflictions will do wonders to help bolster your faith. You may have to wait for it. Remember that the adversity is temporary. It will not last forever. God wants to use it to grow you deep, strengthen your relationships, and draw you closer to Him. He wants to grow you to where He can use you to help others in ways you would never have been able to otherwise. That's right. It's not just about us. We have a tendency to make life too much about "us" and ourselves, searching for worldly happiness and glory for ourselves.

God's message to us and His will for us is that we need to have endurance so that once we have done God's will, we will receive the blessings He has promised. His will: Don't give up, persevere, and trust Him. He promises that if we trust Him, He will accomplish in and through us, His perfect purpose.

Remember that the adversity is temporary. It will not last forever.

We need to be prepared because when we take steps to follow God, things might get worse before they get better. Why, because, as a result, your life is going to make a difference. So, we can expect opposition of all kinds.

Some of the most significant attacks we experience that can have the most devastating impact on us are limiting beliefs that we are "not enough." Our worth is attacked. What we are trying to do "isn't worth anything." When you hear vague putdowns like that in your mind that is condemnation, and you can know it is the enemy trying to discourage you. The Holy Spirit does not condemn. His admonition is always specific—which is conviction—about a particular sin. That is how you can tell the difference.

I know this has been huge for me. I had limiting beliefs about becoming an author. "Who would read anything I wrote? No one even knows who I am." This is where the endurance comes in. The enemy will do his best to impress on your heart that happiness and success are not from God but by any other means. This is when we need to look again in the rear view mirror to see what God has done to carry you through in the past.

He promises that if we trust Him, He will accomplish in and through us, His perfect purpose.

CHAPTER 3

WHAT IS FEAR?

Webster's dictionary defines fear as "an unpleasant, often strong emotion caused by anticipation or awareness of danger, an anxious concern, a reason for alarm, to be afraid or apprehensive."

What are *you* afraid of? What gives *you* anxiety and sleepless nights? Is it your future, your health, your marriage, your children, aging parents, your employment? The list goes on. It's different for everyone. If you are experiencing any form of anxiety, fear, depression, uncertainty, or dread, please realize you are not alone. This is a normal phenomenon that everyone experiences at some point in their life.

We are all "broken" people. Our brokenness just manifests itself in different ways for different people. Above all know this: God loves you in your brokenness and He wants to help. As a child of God in Christ, God Almighty has your back! We must remember the scripture 2 Timothy 1:7 which tells that "God has not given us a spirit of fear but of power and love and self-control.

As a Christ-follower, you have the greatest Father in the universe. Well fathered children are fearless children. The root of all fear, worry, and anxiety is an orphan spirit because orphans are on their own and they have to take care of their own problems and the enemy wants you to feel as though that you're on your own and you have to solve your own problems.

Believe it or not, there is a way to experience peace in the midst of all this and that is what I will be unpacking in this book. We have many choices in life. Every day we're making more choices than we realize. Peace is another choice we can make over fear and anxiety. It takes recognizing where our mind is going and living with the intention to make a U-turn and choosing peace.

That takes focusing on the God who created you, and trusting He is the one in control of all things, even though it may not seem so at times. He lets us experience all kinds of trials and turmoil, and He has His reasons for doing so. If we never had any difficulty, we would feel pretty self-sufficient with no need to turn to Him for guidance and direction.

We need to stop for a second and realize that *no one* really is self-sufficient. Only God is self-sufficient. All we have—even our life—is a gift. We are utterly dependent on Christ for our next breath. We need to understand He has so much more with which He wants to bless us! Did you know that as a Christ-follower we can have access to the wisdom of God? It's true! As a Christ- follower, we have Christ living in us in the form of the Holy Spirit to be the sufficiency for us to have the ability to be content no matter what our circumstances.

> *As a Christ-follower, we have access to the wisdom of God!*

If you look at the Psalms, you will see David and other writers crying out to God in fear, agony, and despair, even asking Him sometimes if He had deserted them because He seemed so far away. When going through something like this, it is easy to get a warped view of God if we are not reading Scripture (the Word of God), and claiming His promises.

He gives us grace in the moment, just when we need it.

Even the Psalms, which can be heavy with honest hopelessness, can be the best antidepressant, full of encouragement at the same time as the psalmists pour out their hearts to God and learn to put their trust in Him. There is no question we are living in very uncertain times of great need, and it is so easy to feel overwhelmed.

You know what? There have always been times like this, which we discover as we study the Scriptures, especially the psalms. I am reminded of where we need to go and who to focus on in times like these. David tells us in Psalm 46:1, "God is our refuge and strength, a very present help in trouble." This whole psalm is a great one to bring comfort when fearful. It starts with this comforting promise and ends with a promise as well as a reminder for us to rest in Him in verse 10, "Be still, and know that I am God."

He is *for* us and wants to be our fortress to provide whatever we need to be comforted. He is our strength—our internal strength to endure. When we are open to Him, He gives us grace in the moment, right when we need it. We don't know what tomorrow holds. All we need to do is to trust Him for today. He tells us in this psalm that He, the Lord our God, is there for us in our time of trouble, our time of need.

During these times of despair, we need to change our perspective to remember the sovereignty of God, and how good, holy, and righteous His is—full of grace, mercy, forgiveness, and truth. We need to trust Him completely, remembering He is faithful, unchanging, and in control, even though it may not seem so. We need to take our eyes off our troubles and remember all the ways God has blessed us and be grateful for the blessings and rainbows we have experienced during our storms. We must realize that if we have big problems, we have a small god. If we have a big God, we will have small problems. If we have a big God, His presence can give us an inner sense of peace, joy, and yes, even contentment during difficult times.

If we have big problems, we have a small god. If we have a big God, we will have small problems.

CHAPTER 4

WHAT IS DEPRESSION?

Let's talk about depression for a minute since it is so rampant and not well understood regarding its causes and remedies. According to Webster's dictionary, depression is "a mood disorder marked especially by sadness, inactivity, difficulty in thinking and concentration, a significant increase or decrease in appetite and time spent sleeping, feelings of dejection and hopelessness, and sometimes suicidal tendencies." It is not necessarily caused by sin, but it can be.

Globally, the World Health Organization (WHO) states that more than 264 million people suffer from depression. However, depression is only one ailment on a long list of diagnosable mental illnesses.

What are some causes for depression? Besides clinical reasons I am not qualified to address, there are two false beliefs that I know of for sure. Some, based on their life-experience and circumstances may believe, "I'm not wanted or needed by anyone. My life has no purpose or meaning. I am a victim of an uncaring world that brings me pain." The other myth causing despair might be the belief that "significance and meaning comes from life and when goals achieved don't bring the happiness expected, there can be a feeling of what's the point of continuing—it's like chasing after the wind."

While we're talking all this doom and gloom, lets' go over some of the symptoms of depression just to make sure we don't leave anyone out. Someone who is depressed may very well have feelings of hopelessness and apathy and find it difficult to concentrate. At the root of depression is a loss of perspective.

There are often physical side effects, including sleeplessness, loss of appetite, or an uncontrollable urge to eat everything in sight. Sometimes there is a loss of sex drive, low self-esteem, desire to withdraw from relationships, fantasy thinking about escaping, and isolating. Occasionally these feelings can include over sensitivity to what others do, inappropriate anger, guilt, and not liking oneself, feeling a need for help, but then feeling even more helpless as others may try to help. Have I covered everyone yet? Have you seen yourself? Are you depressed yet? This is so tragic that anyone would experience *any* of these emotions, but for some they are very real.

Unresolved sin and guilt before God will bring about depression. It might just be the revelation of a need in one's life, the result of which has distorted reality and self-worth. It also can serve as a red flag to indicate help is needed to explore what is amiss. If we recognize and admit our need for help, we can grow from the process. It's essential to be proactive in getting the support we need to resolve these self-defeating emotions; otherwise, they will just fester and grow. How do we safely navigate these landmines of depression?

There are three causes of depression: physical, psychological, and spiritual. If you are clinically depressed, some neurological things are going on in your brain, and clarity is often absent, keeping you from thinking clearly. You could be on antidepressants. The number one drug sold in America is antidepressants. Sometimes medication *is* necessary to help you get your brain back on track so you can start working on your issues.

Multiple physical problems can contribute to depression as well, and even the medications for those medical issues can be a cause for your depression. In these cases, praying isn't the only answer and one should seek professional help. However, we need to be careful not to use medication as an excuse, substitute, or denial for the need to work on our spiritual life to get things right with God. If the underlying causes are not resolved, they may serve as nothing more than a Band-Aid.

Here are some of the primary reasons for depression and the biblical remedy for each:

Cause:	Remedy:
Exhaustion	Rest
Consequences of Sin	Repent
Spiritual Warfare	Resist/Stand Firm/Fight
God's Discipline	Submit to His Pruning
Negative Circumstances	Joyfully Endure

We may ask, "Is depression learned from a family member? Is depression a generational issue? Is its origin genetic? Can it be induced by circumstances or situations in life? Can it be habit forming?" Reverend Nigel Mumford, healing minister and author of *This is Where Your Healing Begins*, would say "Yes to all of the above. Depression can strike whoever....whenever. The good news is, our God is greater!"

Because of something I witnessed recently, I feel the need to include something rather heavy here about depression because it is very real. I will discuss "anxiety" in the next chapter, but I'd like to discuss "angst" right now. Angst is deep anxiety and dread that can migrate into despair and on into depression. Someone who has "angst" about something has an unfocused sense of apprehension of the state of the world and their own future.

Life appears meaninglessness and pointless. Hopelessness sets in with despair and despondency with thoughts that things will never get better. When a person loses hope like that, that is when horrendous things happen. This is not always the case, but many have stated that their hopelessness came from lack of religion and lack of meaning that there is a God and that there something more than themselves.

If someone seems to have become despondent like that and says anything like, "There's no hope" be on high alert. There is a good chance that person has given up on life. I just recently lost a friend to depression and anxiety when she took her life last month. She was saying things like, "This is it. There's no hope." It didn't make sense. All who knew her loved her and her free, loving spirit. While she had experienced some adversity recently, everyone thought she was doing fine.

She was an emotional person—both ways, but had always appeared to be living and loving life. Then a couple of difficult things happened to her and as her husband put it, "She seemed to lose her way and just couldn't find her way back." We all were shocked and saddened greatly by this as you can imagine. I share this because hopelessness really can trigger, especially someone clinically depressed, an emotion that takes them over the edge—so please be aware.

At times, most of us experience episodes of some form of depression, albeit it on a much lesser scale. Most of us experience discouragement, which might turn into the blues, causing us to get depressed and lose perspective. Remember, a certain degree of depression is normal. Even great spiritual leaders can get depressed.

We all have moments and dips in our emotions. If you never had a dip like this, you will at some point, so be prepared so you will know it is just a dip. Don't go down that road of hopelessness. Where do you go when you are discouraged? Be honest and identify that to yourself.

There are varying degrees of depression, so you are not immoral or sinful because you get depressed. Grief over a tragedy or loss of a loved one is a type of depression. Anger turned inward is a huge reason so many people experience depression. If this is a problem for you, then you

The good news is, our God is greater!

need to address and manage that misdirected emotion. If we feel we have been wronged by someone, we must learn the art of forgiveness. That's a whole other topic for another time.

When depressed, there is a tendency to isolate, and that is the worst thing we can do. Even when not experiencing adversity, but especially when we are, we cannot live out our lives in isolation. We need people in our lives with compassionate ears who will not enable us, but allow us to share our struggles and vent if necessary.

If your depression lasts for a long time and moves into suicidal thoughts, losing your appetite, or being unable to get out of bed in the morning, you need to get medical help and see a counselor right away. You should not be alone. Remember, there are three sources of depression: physical, psychological (emotional), and spiritual causes. These are all intertwined and not separate entities. Our emotions are triggered by our thinking and perspective.

Usually, depression begins with wrong, warped thinking. That's why it's so important that as a Christ-follower, we must continually renew our mind by getting into God's Word and spending time in prayer with Him. We need the truth in our lives.

When we find ourselves slipping into that dark corner of depression, we need to remember God's faithfulness in our past. That can be colossal in getting our thinking back on the right track—when we focus on the goodness and faithfulness of God.

Unfortunately, how one reacts to their depression, anxieties, fears, etc. often promotes more of the same. Some are plagued a lot more than others and some have learned to cope better than others, but there is relief for all of us if we know where to look for it.

I have several examples to share and have saved the best for last, so please hang in here with me, and I believe you will find rest for your restless spirit if you apply the lessons that can be gleaned from each of these.

Here is your first story. If you're a Christian, you're probably familiar with the old hymn, "It is Well with My Soul." You may know the story, but it bears repeating, especially if you are not familiar with it. It exemplifies the life of someone who knows how to put their trust in God and can rest in His sovereignty. It also is an example of how someone can have peace in the midst of probably one of the worst nightmares a parent could ever have.

Horatio Spafford was a prominent, successful lawyer in 1871 when the historical Chicago fire destroyed most of his holdings and investments. When the dust settled, he decided he needed to take some time off with his family and go to Europe for a couple of months just to recoup mentally and emotionally from what happened and regain perspective. He booked passage on a boat for himself, his wife, and their four daughters. About the time to leave, he became aware of a zoning problem of some of his properties and decided to stay behind to resolve. So he sent the family ahead and said he would catch the next ship.

The ship carrying his family sank as it was hit by another ship, the *Loch Earn*, and all four daughters drowned. Perhaps you've heard of that famous telegram his wife sent. It simply stated,

"Saved alone." A few weeks later, he boarded a ship to join his wife, and when his ship was crossing the area where the previous ship went down, the captain told Horatio, "This is the place where you lost your daughters."

As he looked over the ocean, with the spirit of God speaking into the deepest part of his soul, he penned the words of that now famous, emotionally stirring hymn. There are six verses to this song that glorify God, and in its entirety it encapsulates the gospel story. For brevity here, I will just quote the first three verses as they explain the point about peace during life's storms. I believe they demonstrate his knowledge of the gospel and his relationship with Christ, which gave him the strength to write these words with such internal conviction and peace. Totally amazing in my mind!

IT IS WELL WITH MY SOUL
By Horatio Spafford

Verse 1:
When peace like a river, attendeth my way.
When sorrows like sea billows roll,
Whatever my lot, Thou has taught me to say,
It is well, it is well with my soul.

(Refrain:)

It is well (it is well) with my soul (with my soul)
It is well, it is well, with my soul

Verse 2:

Though Satan should buffet, though trials should come,
Let this blest assurance control,
That Christ hath regarded my helpless estate,
And hath shed His own blood for my soul.
(Refrain)
Verse 3:
My sin, oh the bliss of this glorious thought!
My sin, not in part, but the whole,
Is nailed to His cross, and I bear it no more,
Praise the Lord, praise the Lord, O my soul!
(Refrain)

This is not theory. This is real stuff we're dealing with here. I'm sure all of us have had a good reason for fear, anxiety, or depression based on our life's experience. If we haven't, we will. It's only a matter of time when we will face some tragedy or challenge in which we will have to choose if we are going to react or respond.

I'm sure we all have experienced the grief of financial loss or the loss of a loved one. What do we do with that? We can drown in despair, or we can choose peace. Let's talk about how to do that, but before we do, I would like to discuss something about which I think a lot of us might identify.

Certainly, this is not always the case, but as I mentioned earlier, our depression can be brought on by unresolved and unconfessed sin in our life. See if you identify with any of this that could be the reason for your depression. That does not have to be the end of it. God, through His Word, tells us how to get through that. Even though God is a forgiving God, we often have to bear the consequences, the ramifications of our sin.

Sometimes personal failure can bring us to the point of deep depression, at least for a time. It may have become such a way of life for you that you don't understand what is going on or why. This is a time of drifting, and one's heart may become hardened. Occasional sins become patterns. Relationships might deteriorate, and guilt may increase. Denial may set in. There may be a tendency to rationalize what you are doing and why, and resort to blame-shifting. You may tend to isolate yourself from people and places that would otherwise bring truth into your life. You might begin to live a life of secrets and lies.

It's possible to be so deep in sin and your conscience so seared you begin to rationalize that it's okay, and if you are a Christ-follower, you may find that your thoughts, words, and actions are no longer congruent with what you know to be true. Our thoughts can easily take us to places we shouldn't go. Toxic thoughts can cloud our thinking and ultimately affect our actions.

If you ever find yourself at this point, you will identify with David in the Bible when he lamented that he felt the heavy hand of God on his life. You see, when you love someone like God loves us, you cannot let them go their own way when it is obviously contrary to the will of God, and that is how God is with us. It is at this point He brings the vice of discipline and love into our lives.

He then brings issues into our life with the intent of getting our attention. If we are dull or stubborn, it might take several different avenues until He has us. When we eventually recognize

He is trying to get our attention, it is only then He can bring truth into our lives as we find ourselves finally receptive. It's at this time God can begin to do a work in us to restore us.

In Psalm 32, David talks about when he was silent about his sin. No one knew besides him, Bathsheba and God. He says his body wasted away, and he groaned all day long. He had been very close to God, but now he felt the "heavy hand of God" upon him—the discipline of what he had done. In other words, he was in a deep depression over his sin. Sometimes the adversity that God brings at a time like this can be very physical. Up to verse five, he did not like himself very much.

In verse five he decided to confess his sin and was forgiven the moment he came clean. Then David talks about the path to restoration, which is available to everyone who follows that same path. It is possible to be in such patterns of denial that you might not hear God's voice initially. You may think you are beyond repair, but if you look at verse eight, God tells you that He will instruct you in how you should go. He is faithful and wants to restore you. If you are genuinely repentant and want that kind of relationship with your Creator, He will not deny you that.

He would rather spend eternity with you than without you. He wants to coach you through to steps of restoration. Guess what? If this is you, you are not the first person to have blown it. I bet you didn't get someone pregnant who was married to a respectable man you had killed to cover up your sin. This was David's story. But once he realized how much he had dishonored God and came clean, God not only forgave him. He called him a man after His own heart. (You can find the story in 2 Samuel 11.)

It is the kindness of the Lord that leads us to repentance. God hates sin, but He never turns down someone who comes to Him with a contrite heart. Someone who owns their stuff, no matter how badly he has blown it, but is deeply sorry for their transgressions, God is always eager to forgive. The Lord is close to the brokenhearted and those with a broken spirit. (Psalm 34:18)

Second Corinthians 10:5 tells us to "take every thought captive to obey Christ." When we do that, we take our focus off ourselves and onto the Lord who is our strength—who promises to meet us wherever we are, to provide whatever we need.

CHAPTER 5

WHAT IS ANXIETY?

According to Merriam-Webster, anxiety is "an apprehensive uneasiness or nervousness, an abnormal and overwhelming sense of apprehension and fear, possibly even mental distress or concern. An anxious individual often anticipates misfortune, danger, or doom."

According to pastor Chip Ingram, the biblical word for anxiety means to "take thought." It can be used positively, like taking thought of something positive, but it usually refers to being obsessed with something that consumes the mind. It is often a fear of a future event, but sometimes it has to do with fear of something happening in the present. It could be anything and will be different for everyone. Another cause of anxiety is the form of regret for an issue that happened in the past.

Ultimately, anxiety causes one to focus on what they cannot control rather than the One who is *in* control. You know you are experiencing anxiety when it causes you to doubt or completely forget about God's power. Not only that, it keeps you from seeking God.

Here are some things anxiety can build up in us, spiritually, mentally, and emotionally. It can make us hyper-alert, irritable, fidgety, talkative, over-dependent; it can give us insomnia, poor memory, fainting episodes, excessive perspiration, muscle tension, headaches, including migraines, a quivering voice, hyperventilation, abdominal pain, nausea, diarrhea, and high blood pressure—to name a few. It can cause one to be paralyzed by fear, possibly causing them to experience a phobia of some kind or another. Wow. I want none of that!

Do you often wake up multiple times during the night and can't sleep, finding it difficult to sleep? Do you find yourself rehashing conversations that you wish could have gone differently? That's caused by anxiety. How do we change any or all of this? We do *not* have to live this way. Jesus promised us that we can absolutely have peace during difficult times.

Jesus promised us that we can absolutely have peace during difficult times.

Pastor Louie Giglio shares about his struggle with anxiety in his book, *Putting An X Through Anxiety*. He came to realize that *his* anxiety wasn't a "thing" in and of itself. Rather it was a symptom of something else. He had a breakthrough when he began to see that something was causing his anxiety, that it was a symptom rather than a cause. He said that sometimes it was something deep within his heart. Sometimes it would be something on the surface of life. But most often he found it was actually a person, not a thing that was causing him to be anxious.

Someone had said or done something that was unsettling to him or the resulting outcome was not what he desired. Most of his anxiety was a result of relationships that were not going well. I honestly think that was my friend's problem. Some relational things had gone wrong in her life and she didn't know how to handle the emotion of it all, and she felt like her life was out of control.

While anxiety can partially be genetically predisposed, it is largely an ingrained learned habit that can be unlearned with the right practices. Anxiety focuses on negativity and limiting beliefs which can be counteracted with practicing gratitude about things for which you really are grateful, no matter how small or insignificant they are.

Eventually, you will find more things you are grateful for until you develop an overall attitude of gratitude. This changes neuropathways, causing a rewiring of your brain from negativity to positivity. Neuroscience has proven this to be effective in literally changing our brain's default position. This is a very simplistic

Whenever God gives us a command, He is always offering us something better.

explanation of a very complex but valuable and well documented process of how we can change our brains.

Once you can put your finger on "what" or "who" is causing this anxiety, robbing you of your peace of mind and even your joy, then you can find yourself on the path to freedom. When you can identify the cause or source of it, you can then specifically cast it on Jesus in a meaningful way. You can transfer the concern and weight of it on Jesus, knowing He cares for you.

In John 14:27, Jesus tells us, "Peace I leave with you; my peace I give to you. Not as the world gives do I give to you. Let not your hearts be troubled, neither let them be afraid." Peter, one of Jesus's disciples, tells us in 1 Peter 5:7, to cast all our anxieties on God because He cares for us. Our God is a personal God who cares for us. He is all-wise, loving, and powerful and believe it or not, we are the object of His affection.

Paul, who wrote over half of the New Testament tells us in Philippians 4:6-7, "Do not be anxious about anything, but in everything by prayer and supplication with thanksgiving let your requests be made known to God. And the peace of God, which surpasses all understanding, will guard your hearts and your minds in Christ Jesus." This is not a condemning reprimand, but an invitation to experience freedom from anxiety. He is not talking about clinical anxiety here.

When He tells us not to be anxious, He doesn't mean we are never to be apprehensive, but not to get stuck there. When we become anxious about anything, we can run into His arms not only for comfort and compassion, but also for guidance and direction in how to deal with whatever our circumstance or need. Whenever God gives us a command, He is always offering us something better.

Through Paul, God is telling us to "Stop worrying." It eats up our soul. It ruins our emotions, thwarts our relationships, and can choke the life out of us. Worry does not empty tomorrow of its sorrow; it empties today of its strength. God never calls us to do something without faithfully enabling us to do it, so He will help you through this.

What does the second part of that verse tell us about how to get out of our misery? He tells us to pray with *gratitude* as we lay out our concerns to Him with the knowledge He will meet us where we are and will provide what we need. You notice it does not necessarily say we will get what we want. Sometimes that is not in our best interests. He knows better than we ever will, what we need, to be who He created us to be. This is where we learn to put our faith and trust in Him. We need to learn how to pray, believing. One thing we can count on is God never made a promise that was too good to be true.

> *Worry does not empty tomorrow of its sorrow; it empties today of its strength.*

When the red light on the dashboard of your car comes on, that is an indication something has gone wrong under the hood. When we lose our peace, that is a red flag—a reliable indicator that something is wrong with our focus and priorities. We are abiding in something other than Christ. The level of our internal peace serves as a monitor or barometer of our relationship to Christ.

By nature, we like to be, or at least think we are in control of things in our life. When life seems to be going out of our control, we tend to comfort ourselves with things that give us a pseudo peace, don't we? It could be a box of chocolates or a bag of chips, a bottle of wine or pills, shopping for things we don't need, or maybe logging onto a website we should avoid. We have a propensity to be drawn to distractions that give us a temporary fulfillment and gratification.

39

But then, the guilt pours in when we realize we have caved to our anxiety inappropriately in a way that has caused more harm than good. The whole thing can become cyclical if we aren't careful. When we do these things, we are not letting the peace of Christ rule in our hearts.

So what do we do when feeling anxious? When anxiety knocks at the door of our heart, let prayer answer it. God tells us that we are to take on an upward focus. It's pausing and remembering who God is and getting a high view of Him. There is a specific way to pray that helps us cover all the bases to pray effectively to give us peace. Someone came up with this acronym to help us remember each step. It's called **ACTS**. I will explain it here.

Worship and **Adoration** is the best way to focus on the goodness of God. Praise Him for His many attributes and character qualities. Then we need to acknowledge that we can't solve our problems on our own and that we need God's help. If we don't admit that we cannot solve our issues, the anxiety will continue to grow. That's where humility kicks in. We call that **Confession**. Then we move into gratitude. Let's call that **Thanksgiving** as we change our focus to God's goodness and His many blessings. It's focusing on the positives and responding with gratitude. Even though things may seem grim at the moment, this is a time to remember His faithfulness in the past. That alone should give us perspective and peace.

God never calls us to do something without faithfully enabling us to do it, so He will help you through this.

Anxiety and thankfulness cannot coexist. After we have done all that, we are to pray for our specific needs asking for a renewed mind so that we can live out what we know to be true of our faithful, loving, gracious God. We call that **Supplication**—praying for our needs and the needs of others.

How do you think our loving God responds when we come to Him in prayer like that trusting Him to meet our needs? Imagine this. When a child is afraid of a storm causing loud, strange noises outside, what does he do? He runs to his parent's room and jumps in bed with them, right? What happens next? Within a couple of minutes, he is breathing heavily, indicating he is asleep, safe in his mother's or father's arms. That is how our heavenly Father wants us to rest in Him. Can you run into His arms and trust Him like an innocent child trusts his parents?

When anxiety knocks at the door of our heart, let prayer answer it.

Living a life of anxiety is not a lifestyle that happens overnight, so we shouldn't expect to suddenly be free from it. Our character is the sum total of our habits. What are habits? They are things we have been doing for so long, that we do them without thinking.

Bad habits that result in poor character need to be changed and that has to be intentional. No way can we live on autopilot and make positive changes in our lives. Changed habits definitely take time and we need to be patient with the journey, realizing that life change generally is not a sprint, but a marathon.

When we live in the flesh, these habits are a dysfunctional drag that counters our ability to flourish and is contrary to the will and kingdom of God. God wants to help with this, but He cannot steer a ship unless it is moving. You have to take those first steps of faith and surrender to a loving God who cares for you even more than a parent cares for their child. Then open your heart in prayer to Him.

Anxiety and thankfulness cannot coexist.

Did you realize you can learn to be content no matter what your circumstances? The New Testament writer Paul came from an affluent background. He was well educated, a Pharisee, highly placed in the Jewish religion. He was a Roman citizen, so pretty much had it made by the world's standards.

Then he met Jesus in a vision on the road to Damascus where he was on his way to persecute the "Christ-followers" of his day. After that, he renounced all that he had, took on a Christ-follower mission that resulted in his being homeless, beaten within an inch of his life several times, even left for dead once, shipwrecked, and imprisoned numerous times. Yet he said he had learned to be content whatever his circumstances because he was serving the living Christ, and that was all the mattered to him. Contentment is something we learn.

He tells us in Philippians 4:11-13, "Not that I am speaking of being in need, for I have learned in whatever situation I am to be content. I know how to be brought low, and I know how to abound. In any and every circumstance, I have learned the secret of facing plenty and hunger, abundance, and need. I can do all things through Him who strengthens me."

I have heard so many people say, "If this or that happens, then I'll be happy." It's all based on circumstances. Once they get the coveted achievement, then I so often hear something like, "That's it? Is that all there is?" Jim Carey, the comedic celebrity, once said "I think everybody should get rich and famous and do everything they ever dreamed of so they can see that it's not the answer."

I heard of a reporter who went to interview Muhammed Ali at his farmhouse, and Ali gave the reporter a tour. They ended up in his barn where all his trophies, ribbons, and memorabilia were showcased on the shelves gathering dust and even pigeon droppings. Ali softly said, "I had the world, I had *all* the world, and it was nothin'." So often, I think we place too much importance on what other people think rather than what God thinks. Who really should matter in the long run?

I just quoted from Philippians, chapter 4, in which a few verses earlier, Paul tells us to be anxious for nothing, but with thanksgiving, we are to go to God in prayer with our needs. The book of Philippians is a letter he wrote to the congregation of a church he had started in Philippi, Greece. It has become known as the "epistle of joy" because Paul refers to the joy of the Lord as his strength, giving him peace. Paul wrote this letter when he was in prison, so I would say he had mastered what it was like to rest in Jesus, who gave him the peace and joy he could never have experienced without learning how to be content whatever his circumstances.

Contentment is not something to achieve; it is a secret to be discovered. We can learn so much from Paul. We need to learn that internal peace and contentment is not dependent on our circumstances, but from dependence on Christ, who is our peace and gives us all things.

This is not pretending that everything in our life is perfect when it's not. It's not about ignoring genuine hurt, heartache, pain, grief, or disappointment. It's not about denying struggles and suffering in this world. It *does* say that we can have perpetual joy, peace, comfort, strength, and contentment in the middle of the pain.

There is a contentment that is entirely free from all those circumstances. We must guard ourselves from thinking we can muster up this contentment on our own. This type of mindset is why self-help books centered around positive thinking abound. Many think it's just a matter of self-talk, self-worth and self-sufficiency with positive thinking that will bring about contentment. Please hear me. That is not contentment. Instead, it is conceit to think we can muster this up on our own. Self-focus, in any way, is pride.

A couple of questions we occasionally need to ask ourselves are 1) what am I focusing on—what I do have vs. what I don't, and 2) am I teachable? Besides the verses I have already shared, we need to memorize a couple more. Paul reminds us in 1Thessalonians 5:16-18, "Rejoice always, pray without ceasing, give thanks in all circumstances; for this is the will of God in Christ Jesus for you." We need to ask God what He wants us to learn, rather than telling Him what we want Him to change. Then we need to ask Him what needs to change in our lives so we can be more like Christ. If you did that, would that change your prayer life?

I know it seems like an oxymoron, but if we take the focus off ourselves and look with compassion as to how we can help others, that will bring us more contentment than the greed of always getting what we think we want and need. It is very counter-intuitive, but you have heard it is in giving that we receive— and the measure with which we give is used to give back to us. So, if we give little, we will get little. If we give a lot, we receive a lot. Whatever we need, plant a seed. But be careful. Never give with the motive to get. Just give, and you *will* get in ways you never anticipated.

> *Contentment is not something to achieve; it is a secret to be discovered.*

My pastor, David Platt defines contentment this way, "Contentment is the sweet inward state of perpetual joy, peace, gentleness, and strength in every moment regardless of our circumstances." Let's unpack that a bit in the next section

CHAPTER 6

WHAT IS GOD'S AGENDA FOR US?

Believe it or not, God's primary plan is not to make us happy, but to make us more like His Son. That should be the goal of every Christ-follower—to be imitators of Him. How we respond to difficult circumstances gives us who follow Christ a platform to show how He makes a difference in our lives.

Who was Christ? Among many other things, like saving us for eternity, we can point to Him as a role model in so many ways. We see He was full of grace and mercy, filled with humility as He exemplified the integrity of a servant leader, who led by example, showing compassion even to those who opposed Him. We can actually thank Him for our ups and downs because we know He has an overall positive plan for our lives. We learn on this journey that prosperity does not have the power to give us contentment; neither does poverty have the ability to take it away.

> *Our brain will not allow us to be grateful and discontent at the same time, so we have to make a choice.*

It is amazing how our life can change when we make gratitude for what we do have our focus. It creates a heart change that can overcome about any adversity, and only Christ can give us what we need to overcome any difficult circumstances in life. Unbelievers tend to think that getting "things" will bring them contentment. The only problem is that when the goal is achieved, as we have discovered, it doesn't deliver the expected gratification.

It's very easy if we are not careful even as believers also to turn inward, chase a dream and think it's Jesus *plus* other things we desire that will bring us fulfillment. We can just as quickly get caught up in the lie that contentment comes from specific achievements or getting *stuff*. This is a pervasive lie that many of us have embraced, and has contributed to a boon in Christian counselling because of the remorse and depression that follows our failure.

Contentment does not come from independence, but total dependence on Christ. We must learn to believe the truth of the verse above: Philippians 4:13, "I can do all things through Him who gives me strength." That means Christ plus nothing.

What would it look like if your circumstances had no power over your ability to experience contentment and peace? At the end of this great letter to the Philippian church Paul is trying to encourage, he says in 4:19, "And my God will supply every need of yours according to his riches in glory in Christ Jesus" (NIV). I quote that knowing we

> *What would it look like if your circumstances had no power over your ability to be content and at peace?*

sometimes get our wants and needs mixed up, but God doesn't, and He knows exactly what we need. The way we experience God's promises is to trust Him.

CHAPTER 7

HOW SHOULD WE DEAL
WITH FEAR AND ANXIETY?

How do we overcome this fear that wants to grip our hearts? If you are a Christ-follower, you will know the Bible tells us in many places that we are to "Fear not." We know Christ is with us; in fact, He is *in* us in the person of the Holy Spirit to give us peace during difficult and uncertain times. Jesus provides the answer to our fear. If you are not a Christ-follower *YET,* I hope you will hear me out because this book will give you hope and even change your life if you let it, so please keep an open mind as you read this and let the truth of it permeate your unsettled spirit.

One thing to keep in mind is that "where focus goes, energy flows and becomes our reality." So, we need to decide what we are going to focus on, the positive or negative, in every situation. Is our focus on Jesus and what He offers us when we put our trust in Him, or is our focus on the world and its uncertainties? I don't mean to minimize all that is going on. We cannot control it for sure, but we can control how we respond to it. This mentality translates to anything negative that might be going on in our lives, not just this scary

Where focus goes, energy flows and becomes our reality

virus, but any negative situations that could take us down if we let them. Are we going to respond or to react? These are actually two very different things.

We can choose to be grateful for what we do have and what's going on in our life that is good, or we can choose to focus on the negative and what we don't have. We cannot do both at the same time. Our brain will not allow us to be grateful and discontent simultaneously so we have to choose. Life is full of choices. We can choose to make the best out of any situation in which we find ourselves, or we can choose to give in to fear and anxiety.

If we let it, adversity can be a bridge that brings us to a deeper relationship with God

We have nothing to fear if we put our trust in the God who saved us. The psalmist David reminds us in Psalm 27:1, "The Lord is my light and my salvation, whom shall I fear? The LORD is the stronghold of my life- of whom shall I be afraid?"

God, through the prophet Isaiah in Isaiah 41:10 also tells us, "Do not fear, for I am with you; do not be dismayed, for I am your God. I will strengthen you and help you; I will uphold you with my righteous right hand." What we focus on in uncertain times matters.

Remember, in Matthew 14:28-31, when Peter went to walk on the water, and took his eyes off Jesus and looked down and waves? What happened when he took his focus off Christ? He started to drown, didn't he? Remember also in Mark 4:37-40 when Jesus was asleep in the boat, and the storm came up suddenly, and the disciples were afraid of capsizing? The only time Jesus ever really rebuked them was when they showed their unbelief, and lack of faith in Him to take care of them.

Jesus expects us to trust Him when the wind and waves of misfortune confront us. If we let it, adversity can be a bridge that brings us to a deeper relationship with God. We also need to keep in mind that while we may feel like we are experiencing a tsunami in our life right now, if it were not for storms, there would be no rainbows.

Fear, panic, and anxiety are emotions rooted in all the negative "what ifs" that *might* happen in the future. This could encompass any number of things, including financial loss, relationship crises, physical harm, or worry over any negative possibilities that *could* happen.

I want to share a portion of Scripture with you here. It's rather long, but it is powerful. I love the whole section, and it will make sense when I share the following story with you. It's from Matthew 6:25-34.

> *While we may feel like we are experiencing a tsunami in our life right now, if it were not for storms, there would not be rainbows.*

Therefore I tell you, do not be anxious about your life, what you will eat or what you will drink, nor about your body, what you will put on. Is not life more than food, and the body more than clothing? Look at the birds of the air: they neither sow nor reap nor gather into barns, and yet your heavenly Father feeds them. Are you not of more value than they? And which of you by being anxious can add a single hour to his span of life? And why are you anxious about clothing? Consider the lilies of the field, how they grow: they neither toil nor spin, yet I tell you, even Solomon in all his glory was not arrayed like one of these. But if God so clothes the grass of the field, which today is alive and tomorrow is thrown into the oven, will he not much more clothe you, O you of little faith? Therefore do not be anxious, saying, "What shall we eat?" or "What shall we drink?" or "What shall we wear?" For the Gentiles seek after all these things, and your heavenly Father knows that you need them all. But seek first the kingdom of God and his righteousness, and all these things will be added to you. Therefore do not be anxious about tomorrow, for tomorrow will be anxious for itself. Sufficient for the day is its own trouble.

CHAPTER 8

WHAT I LEARNED ABOUT FEAR

When my mother was diagnosed with Alzheimer's disease, I was fearful she might end up like my neighbor who had it for many years and turned into an extremely mean-spirited, high maintenance, nasty woman. My mom had always been so sweet, easygoing, and submissive. I knew if she turned out like this woman, it would be emotionally draining and challenging for my dad, who was her primary caregiver during her final years.

They had always had a close, loving relationship, and I dreaded for my dad to have to experience and put up with that type of behavior. I shared my fears with a friend I highly respected—about the same age as my mom. She urged me *not* to be fearful of what *might* happen because it may never happen. "Why worry about something that has not yet happened?" she told me. "It may never happen, and then you will have worried yourself sick over nothing. If it does happen, you will know it's not your mom acting that way. It's the disease." She also gave me some Scriptures to encourage me the area of fear.

Why worry about something that has not yet happened

53

Alzheimer's is a dreadful disease and it hurt terribly to see a formerly articulate woman who had many published articles, who spoke frequently to women's groups and was a soloist in church, lose all of that. However, she never did act out like my neighbor. She kept her sweet demeanor until the end. I won't deny it was painful to core to see such an intellectual decline of the mother I loved so much and while I experienced many difficult emotions during that time, fear was not one of them.

I was glad I listened to my mature friend, and I always remembered that valuable lesson I learned about worry and fear. Twenty-six years later, I still remembered this lesson when confronted with another opportunity to resort to fear, but based on what I learned from her and the Scriptures, I chose not to.

AN EXAMPLE OF GOD'S GRACE AND PROVISION

I was holding the ladder for my husband, who was doing some repairs on our portico over our front porch, when he missed the top rung on his way down, flipped and fell headfirst around twelve feet. He landed on the top of his head on the edge of our flagstone steps and his head split open, right there in front of me. Blood was pouring out from this huge gash, and we found out later he had severed an artery.

In the emergency room, it became quickly apparent all the medical staff were concerned about paralysis. They kept asking him to wiggle his fingers and toes and asked if he had any tingling or numbness. Every person who came into the room asked the same questions. Bob had never lost consciousness and had been moving around, so I hadn't even thought about paralysis. All I could think about was brain injury or brain trauma because of the long, large split in the top and down the back of his head that was so visible. He ended up with around eighty stitches in his head.

When they started asking about the movement and feeling of his appendages, I realized the concern about paralysis was very real. I could have gone directly to fear at that moment, but I resolved not to. It had not yet happened, and it might not. If it did, we would deal with it, but for now, I was not going to go there—thanks to the lesson I learned twenty-six years ago from my friend. I had a surprising, unexplainable calm through all of this. A CAT scan revealed Bob had broken his neck—shattering his C1, which is the atlas that holds the head onto the spinal column. He had fractured the occipital lobes of his skull and several other vertebrae as well from the impact.

I was told he was going to have to be transferred, by ambulance, to another hospital that had a trauma unit, which meant moving him from gurney to gurney to gurney. His condition was so fragile, one false move might be all it would take to result in paralysis. I was praying under my breath everything would be okay in that a surgeon would hopefully be able to fuse his head to his spinal column. While he would have to adjust to a new normal with limited mobility,

"Lord, however this turns out, let it be for your glory."

I prayed he would not become paralyzed. I didn't know until later Bob had prayed in the first ER before the CAT scan, "Lord, however this turns out, let it be for your glory." God answered that prayer.

Because of the location of his injury, if he *were* paralyzed, he would have been a quad—worst-case scenario, besides death. We have shown the surgeon's report to doctors, chiropractors, and imaging specialists, who have all said, "No one walks away with an injury like this." But, by the grace of God, He did. Our one friend, who is a doctor, told us when he saw the report, he wept because he was sure Bob was going to be paralyzed. The physician's assistant said they perform very few surgeries like his because usually, people don't survive a fall like that, with his type of injury. My husband is a walking miracle.

Let me just back up to say I cannot take credit for the strength I experienced during this time. Of course, I was extremely concerned about the fate of my husband. He is the love of my life, and we have been married for over 40 years. I want to give you an example of God's grace and how He is always with us, giving us exactly what we need when we need it in the way of comfort and care. We just must recognize it. Sometimes we see it not in the moment, but in retrospect. He is there nonetheless, giving just the amount of necessary grace we need in the moment, and He is always on time.

Remember, how in Exodus, God spoke to Moses from the burning bush, "God said to him, 'I AM WHO I AM.' He said, Say this to the people of Israel: 'I AM has sent me to you.'" Later, in the book of John, in the New Testament, Jesus said that same thing about Himself, that He was the "I Am." Many see that as God is all-sufficient, He "*IS*" whatever we need Him to be for us. (I Am = He is...) *HE* is all we need.

At any rate, God was my strength during this difficult time of uncertainty. Everything happened so fast that I hadn't even had time yet to tell my family or friends about it or ask them to pray for us. But, what's so amazing, as we looked back over this, we realized that God is not constrained by time (2 Peter 3:8), and He knew beforehand that hundreds of prayers would be lifted up on our behalf. He answered

> *God was my strength during this difficult time of uncertainty*

them even before they were prayed. How awesome is that?

While we were in the first ER, I group texted our three grown kids. "Pray for Dad, Bad fall off ladder. In ER." Then on my way to join the ambulance and the new medical team at a different hospital across town, I called a good friend to please send a mass email to a large list of our friends. We are involved in several ministries, so we have access to several large email lists. Word like this travels fast, and within the hour, over five hundred people were notified of the accident, and prayers were shooting up to heaven like clusters of arrows on our behalf.

My daughter is the "Facebook queen," so in no time she had posted the need for prayer on her timeline and tagged Bob and Me so that both of our feeds were alerted. Who knows how many additional people were praying from that announcement. We have never been the recipient of so many prayers, and it was humbling.

Our kids are scattered across the US, but all dropped everything and came as fast as they could to be with their dad and support me. The friend I called met me at the second ER to comfort me. Her husband left work and joined us as well. In no time, two of my husband's best friends were by his side in the ER while we waited for a room.

> *Sometimes, besides showing up in our spirit to give us strength, God uses other people in our lives to tangibly support and minister to us in our time of need as well.*

Sometimes, besides showing up in our spirit to give us strength, God uses other people in our lives to tangibly support and minister to us in our time of need as well. We need to remember that because we may be tempted while going through a difficult time to ask God where He is. He may very well be there in the form of a friend giving us "in-person" comfort. In our situation, we experienced it all. I don't know when I have ever felt more cared for and loved.

CHAPTER 9

WHERE IS GOD DURING CHALLENGING TIMES?

I know that God does not always answer our prayers in the way that we want, but He is still there with us during the storms of life to get us through them. Thankfully for us, this was a time when He answered our prayers the way we hoped, and we will be eternally grateful for that.

Even if the results had not turned out so positive for us, He still is a good God who always has our best interests at heart, and He will not waste experiences. There are always lessons we can learn in all our life experiences, especially the hard ones, if we are open to learning what they are. Besides that, based on His promises in the Bible, we can be assured that He will be with us, walking through the storms of life with us. He will never leave us or forsake us (Hebrews 13:5).

Sometimes, as an answer to prayer, He will solve our problems for us, but most of the time, He wants us to be aware of His presence and to be mindful of Him carrying us through them.

Sometimes, as an answer to prayer, He will solve our problems for us, but most of the time, He wants us to be aware of His presence and to be mindful of Him carrying us through them. He wants us to rest in Him. There is a famous poem you are probably familiar with, but it seems appropriate to share it here as it fits in well with our discussion about God's presence during hardship.

FOOTPRINTS IN THE SAND
By Mary Stevenson (1936)

One night I dreamed a dream.

As I was walking along the beach with my Lord,
Across the dark sky flashed scenes from my life.

For each scene, I noticed two sets of footprints in the sand, One belonging to me and one to my Lord.

After the last scene of my life flashed before me,
I looked back at the footprints in the sand.

I noticed that at many times along the path of my life, especially at the very lowest and saddest times, there was only one set of footprints.

This really troubled me, so I asked the Lord about it.

"Lord, you said once I decided to follow you,
You'd walk with me all the way.

But I noticed that during the saddest and most troublesome times of my life, there was only one set of footprints.

I don't understand why, when I needed You the most, You would leave me."

He whispered, "My precious child, I love you and will never leave you.

Never, ever, during your trials and testings.
When you saw only one set of footprints,
It was then that I carried you."

He tells us to lean on Him. "Come to me, all who labor and are heavy laden, and I will give you rest. Take my yoke upon you, and learn from me, for I am gentle and lowly in heart, and you will find rest for your souls. For my yoke is easy, and my burden is light" (Matthew 11:28-30).

He wants us to rest in Him, to trust in Him, knowing His ways are better than our ways, and His thoughts greater than our thoughts (Isaiah 55:9). He knows so much better what we need than we do. He wants to bless us, but sometimes we have to go through a process of surrender and obedience before experiencing those blessings.

Sometimes we have to go through a process of surrender and obedience before experiencing those blessings.

61

CHAPTER 10

ARE YOU FEARFUL OF YOUR FUTURE?

When our focus is on all that could possibly go wrong in the things mentioned above, fear will most likely rear its ugly head. When Jesus was talking with His disciples in the upper room, just before He went to the Garden of Gethsemane to be arrested and taken to the cross, He told them some difficult things. He expressed that even though He was about to face death and they persecution and some even death, that they need not be afraid. "Let not your hearts be troubled. Believe in God; believe also in me. In my Father's house are many rooms. If it were not so, would I have told you that I go to prepare a place for you?" (John 14:1-2).

He promised them they would live in a world of tribulation, difficulty, and persecution, but He told them, "I have said these things to you, that in me you may have peace. In the world you will have tribulation. But take heart; I have overcome the world" (John 16:33).

If you are a Christ-follower, you understand perfect love casts out fear (1 John 4:18). If you have experienced the saving grace and love of Jesus Christ, you know it is possible to experience peace when we encounter the storms of life. We are in a position to model calm and confidence in a loving, caring God, knowing He is sovereign, He's in control, and He has our back. He is faithful and unchanging and having our best interest in mind, He will provide what we need when we need it. Faith in our faithful God allows us to live fearlessly and to show how He equips us no matter what we might face during uncertain times. "In the same way, let your light shine before others, so that they may see your good works and give glory to your Father who is in heaven" (Mathew 5:16).

Faith in our faithful God allows us to live fearlessly and to show how He equips us no matter what we might face during uncertain times.

Do you ever wonder, "Where is God" when going through challenging times? Does He seem distant or even non-existent? What is the biggest crisis you are experiencing right now?

While you're thinking about that, I will attempt to unpack and explain a psalm that is so familiar that there is a tendency to gloss over it and think, "Oh, I know that psalm. I even memorized it as a child. It's usually read at funerals." Well, I bet there is so much more to this psalm than you ever imagined. At least that's what I discovered when the twenty-third psalm was explained to me by an actual shepherd, Phillip Keller, in his book, *A Shepherd Looks at the 23ʳᵈ Psalm*. Keller was a sheepherder for over a decade in the hills of Australia.

This is going to take a while, so why don't you grab a cup of your favorite beverage and get comfortable, as I take my time to go into detail why understanding this psalm may help you appreciate your Shepherd's heart and how He can help you get through your current valley or storm. Let's be clear that this was written as a metaphor. As you read my descriptions of the sheep and shepherd, to get the lessons from this message, please continuously think about the correlation between us as the sheep and God as the shepherd. See if you can find all the connections.

First of all, I will provide it below so you can review it, or if you don't know it, you can follow along. I'm taking this from the English Standard Translation (ESV), as that is my favorite. As you read it, notice how personal and intimate it is with all the personal pronouns, "I," "me," and "my."

THE LORD IS MY SHEPHERD
A Psalm of David (Psalm 23)

*The LORD is **my** shepherd; **I** shall not want.*
*He makes **me** lie down in green pastures.*
*He leads **me** beside still waters.*
*He restores **my** soul.*
*He leads **me** in paths of righteousness for his name's sake.*

*Even though **I** walk through the valley of the shadow of death,*
***I** will fear no evil, for you are with **me**;*
*your rod and your staff, they comfort **me**.*

*You prepare a table before **me** in the presence of **my** enemies;*

*you anoint **my** head with oil; **my** cup overflows.*
*Surely goodness and mercy shall follow **me** all the days of*
my life,
*and **I** shall dwell in the house of the LORD forever.*

At the time this was written, readers would have understood the metaphor as they could relate, understanding sheep and the shepherd's role. In America, most of us are not that knowledgeable about sheep or shepherding, so we need an explanation.

Many times throughout scripture, we are referred to as sheep. It's not complimentary, but rather than be offended, let's see if we can learn why we are compared to them. First of all, let's understand a few things about sheep. They are slow, defenseless, and dumb, to put it bluntly. They are defenseless as they are afraid of their own shadow. Without help, they cannot find food or water and won't drink from a babbling brook because they are afraid of its noise. That's why a shepherd will often dam up an area of a stream, creating "still waters" where he can then guide the sheep to drink.

Rather than looking for greener, fresher grass, they'll eat grass down to the roots, ruining the pasture, and unless the shepherd guides or leads them to fresh grass, they'll die. If they happen to end up on their back, they cannot get up without help from the shepherd. Basically, sheep are helpless without a shepherd and so are we.

The shepherd was the lowliest job there was. It was always the youngest son's job to care for the sheep. They were to carry a "rod" in their belt, which was used to slay or scare off any predator trying to harm or take away their sheep. They also would carry the "staff," which was used to guide the wandering sheep back into the fold or lift it out of a bush or ravine where they had wandered off and gotten stuck. Occasionally they might even give them a little rap on the behind with it to let them know they had gone astray and were not to do that.

Here's another great lesson. If a sheep continually wandered away, the shepherd, to protect the sheep from getting lost and therefore die, would purposely break the sheep's leg, lovingly put it in a splint and then carry it around his neck so that they could bond, while the wound healed. When the bone had healed, the shepherd would put a little bell around that sheep's neck, and he would be called the bell sheep. He would stay close to the shepherd, and the other sheep would hear that bell and would follow.

There are many names for God, like Yahweh and Jehovah, but the Good Shepherd is also one of them. He is Eternal, Creator, the list goes on. Remember earlier, I referred to God as the "I Am." He is any, all, and everything we will ever need. You notice David starts this psalm, "The Lord is *My* Shepherd." The fact he referred to God as "my" Shepherd made it one of the most intimate, personal names we have for God. In his day, they understood a good shepherd protects, provides, and cares for his sheep. He understands, nourishes, and loves his sheep. It's a humble, lowly, serving job.

Here we have sheep described as very vulnerable, but they also are very valuable. They provide sustenance (milk and lamb for food), and they can be sheared. Their wool can be sold to provide for other family needs.

Compared to the goodness of God, we are like sheep. When it comes to living life in light of eternity, we can be as dumb as sheep. We can be as vulnerable as they are, but to God, we also are valuable. The Good Shepherd is not a God who is way out there, shaking His finger when we mess up. He is a God who intimately cares about each one of us.

If you look closely at the way this psalm reads, there are some statements about the present, but several about the future, which shows David's confidence in God's continued provision. We can learn how to be just as confident in God providing what we need, especially if we look at how He has done so in the past.

Now let's walk through this and see if we can learn what David understood about his Great Shepherd. He starts out saying he has no wants because his Shepherd will provide all his needs. I spoke earlier about the fact that we have physical, psychological (emotional), and spiritual needs and that they are all intertwined. Here David tells us his Shepherd meets *all* his needs. He has *no* wants. He doesn't necessarily meet y*our* wants or y*our* agenda, but He promises to meet your physical, psychological, and spiritual needs all the days of your life. He can do that only if you *let* Him be *your* Shepherd.

"He restores my soul." Restore here means to repent or even to be converted, giving grace. He puts back and holds together.

He holds us up, much like with an invisible hand. Soul here refers to our psyche. As for spiritual issues, He guides and gives direction, putting us on the right path.

The other option is to think you are a pretty big sheep (feeling somewhat self-sufficient) with pretty good (reasonable, logical) ideas and the ability to handle things on your own—to graze where *you* think *you* will be fulfilled. You think you prefer to find water and live life on your terms. What happens when a real sheep thinks that way? It's a disaster for him, isn't it?

Our problem is that deep down, we are proud and arrogant. We want to be our own sheep and our own shepherd. Grace always follows humility, but humility is hard for human sheep to swallow—to admit our need.

This does not just apply to Old Testament times. I hope you see the connection here about a shepherd and our Shepherd. To come full circle—back to Paul in the New Testament, remember his exhortation in Philippians 4:19, "And my God will supply every need of yours according to his riches in glory in Christ Jesus."

What was true then is true now. Whatever your crisis, if you bring your life under the leadership and Lordship of the Shepherd, He will be there to meet your needs. He may not meet them your way or on your time-table, but you can be sure it will be the best for you in the long run. He may have to do some work *in* you

> *Grace always follows humility, but humility is hard for human sheep to swallow—to admit our need.*

He may have to do some work in you before He can work through you, but as long as you are open to Him, He has promised to meet you.

before He can work *through* you, but as long as you are open to Him, He has promised to meet you.

When David says he is not afraid of evil, he means harm of any sort. How can he say that? Because he has confidence his Shepherd is *with* him and will protect him from *all* evil of any kind. So the Shepherd is not just a provider but also the protector. He says, "Your rod and your staff, they comfort me." He is there to protect us from the enemy and others who might harm us or lead us astray. But sometimes, He might even have to protect us from ourselves.

Whether we want to acknowledge it or not, there is an invisible war going on through which the enemy wants desperately to tempt you to get your focus off God and onto yourself and your current difficult circumstances. He wants to fill your heart with fear, doubt, and overwhelming anxiety. His goal is to destroy you, and that can manifest itself in many different ways. You may find yourself getting angry and giving in where you are most vulnerable.

At the same time, however, if you are a Christ-follower, the Holy Spirit inside you wants to turn that same temptation into a trial He can use for your good as you learn to let Him be your provider and protector. When seen as a trial, you can see by faith that God has allowed it to provide an opportunity to persevere, thereby increasing your confidence as it was intended for your growth. By faith, you can choose to consider it all joy, and as you endure it, God's character is developed, and your life is transformed more into the image of Christ.

Character enlarges us, making us bigger than our circumstances would naturally allow. It also purifies us. It is not something we are born with. It has to be developed. (As an interesting side note, our character also is the only thing we take with us when we die.)

> *You can, by faith choose to consider it all joy, and as you endure it, God's character is developed and your life is transformed more into the image of Christ.*

The most resilient and those who handle adversity the best, are those who have experienced it at some level when they are young and learned how to negotiate, overcome, and endure it.

If you should need a little shot in the arm concerning the benefits of trials, read the first chapter of James in the New Testament. Here is an excerpt from James 1:2-8:

> Count it all joy, my brothers, when you meet trials of various kinds, for you know that the testing of your faith produces steadfastness. And let steadfastness have its full effect, that you may be perfect and complete, lacking in nothing. If any of you lacks wisdom, let him ask God, who gives generously to all without reproach, and it will be given him. But let him ask in faith, with no doubting, for the one who doubts is like a wave of the sea that is driven and tossed by the wind. For

71

that person must not suppose that he will receive anything from the Lord; he is a double-minded man, unstable in all his ways.

Then James 1:12-14 says:

Blessed is the man who remains steadfast under trial, for when he has stood the test he will receive the crown of life, which God has promised to those who love him. Let no one say when he is tempted, "I am being tempted by God," for God cannot be tempted with evil, and he himself tempts no one. But each person is tempted when he is lured and enticed by his own desire. Then desire when it has conceived gives birth to sin, and sin when it is fully grown brings forth death.

Don't give in, give up, or let go. This crisis you are going through now, or any dilemma you may have in the future, may make you more like Jesus than you have ever known, or it could pull you entirely away from Him. The choice is yours.

We're not finished with this psalm yet. We are now at the part where David says, "Even though I walk through the valley of the shadow of death, I will fear no evil." Sometimes a shepherd has to take the sheep through some terrain of ravines and valleys to where there is fresh, lush grass. When they have to walk through these ravines between two mountains, the shadows cause darkness, and that is where a shepherd will most likely lose some sheep. Predators seem to know they can go there undetected. So this metaphor illustrates for us, any darkness, any crisis, the darkest of times, or fear of the unknown. David reminds us that we don't need to be afraid because the Good Shepherd is with us. As they passed through that hazardous area, the shepherd would gather the sheep in close to himself to protect them.

No matter what our darkness, we can count on His presence. Do you remember when Paul was suffering from some sort of physical affliction, and he asked God three times to remove it from him, but God said, "No?" Sometimes, when God has bigger plans than ours, He will say, "No." Remember, His ways are not our ways (Isaiah 55:8).

In Paul's case, God added, "My grace is sufficient for you." Paul then went on to say in the same verse (2 Corinthians 12:9), "Therefore I will boast all the more gladly of my weaknesses, so that the power of Christ may rest upon me."

This crisis you are going through right now, or any dilemma you may have in the future, may make you more like Jesus than you have ever known, or it could pull you completely away from Him. The choice is yours.

God tells us if we come, wherever we are, He'll meet us there and give us just enough grace for that moment.

Remember, we said the rod was to fight off the enemy? Whenever you are in the dark times of your life, then that is when the enemy will swoop in and throw lies at you and cause you to experience all kinds of limiting beliefs. The wrong voices in your head will encourage you to take shortcuts that will take you down paths of destruction.

Our Shepherd has a rod to take down the enemy. In Ephesians 6:10-18, God, through Paul, tells us that we have armor and weaponry (in Him) to protect us with His power. As we go through a difficult time, we have to realize God has a game plan bigger than us to get us through it.

No matter what our darkness, we can count on His presence.

He may be pruning us. What happens when trees and bushes are pruned? New growth is stimulated, and they are reshaped to be more beautiful than if left alone, aren't they? He may need to prune us, to change us, and you can be sure it will be for the better.

When life is running smoothly, we aren't exactly seeking God for counsel are we, especially compared to when we are down. We tend to forget God when things are running effortlessly, don't we? It's during the dark times that, if we seek God, we will surely find Him waiting with open arms to be what we need Him to be in that moment. We do not have to be "in want" because our great Shepherd will meet all our needs. While we may experience some degree of fear, we are not to be paralyzed by it.

At this point in the psalm, David changes the metaphor of his culture, celebrating who God is to a banquet or rejoicing. Banquets were lavish celebrations, often after a victorious battle— a demonstration of deliverance. Food and drink would flow freely while the defeated enemy would be forced to watch this celebration. It was a great time of fellowship and merriment.

Here he refers to the joy of experiencing the abundant, eternal life in the present, not just in the afterlife. This is relating to a spilling over of joy from the inside out—an assurance in an abundant life now and forever—a confident trust in the Great Shepherd regardless of circumstances, no matter how grim they may seem to be. Inside, there is a life overflowing with that inner joy and peace that can only come from the Great Shepherd.

God tells us that if we come, wherever we are, He'll meet us there and give us just enough grace for that moment.

In biblical times, battles between nations were over a conflict of deities. Pagans worshipped many gods, and this celebration was to honor the true God and show off their victory as proof their God was bigger and better than their gods.

CHAPTER 11

WHAT NOW?

Our biggest and worst battle is not a struggle with finances, relationships, or even cancer—whatever we think is our primary concern. It's sin. We are a slave to whatever we obey. Left to ourselves, we are slaves to sin. We can be a slave to sin or a servant of Christ. If we become servants of Christ, that lifestyle change and "end of life assurance" from that ownership change are incomprehensible.

The abundant life is characterized by peace, and that is what seems to be elusive when we are caught up in our sin of trying to live life on our terms and the self-sufficiency of trying to be self-reliant (a big sheep) with our agenda.

Peace comes from salvation—deliverance from our enemy—in our case, our sin. Romans 5:1 tells us, "Therefore, since we have been justified by faith, we have peace with God through our Lord Jesus Christ." You notice that is present tense "have" peace with God. This isn't just for when we die. It is for now and forever.

We are a slave to whatever we obey

77

Before We Wrap This Up, Let's Look at One More Verse—Philippians 4:4

"Rejoice in the Lord always; again I will say rejoice." I think Paul repeated himself because he felt it was crucial and wanted to be sure that we "got it." We are to rejoice always in all things. This is something we cannot do in our efforts. It is only possible through the power of the Holy Spirit. Joy is not a personality type; it's a command. As Christ-followers, we are commanded to display the "Fruit of the Spirit" in our lives, and joy is just one of them. It's not merely a feeling. Rejoicing is something we do. Joy doesn't always feel like happiness.

We need to give others, even ourselves, space and the grace to be sorrowful sometimes. When tragedies happen in our lives, as I've already mentioned, it's okay to grieve. The important lesson we can learn from Paul is that while we may be sorrowful over something, we can be rejoicing at the same time. Remember, joy does not always feel like happiness. There is a way to rejoice in the midst of our sadness.

Joy is not dependent on circumstances

It is not inappropriate or impossible. Its source is an inner strength that can only come from the Holy Spirit within us. If you do not have the Holy Spirit in your life, you cannot experience the kind of joy at the level I am speaking of here.

Sometimes, rejoicing in the Lord during a time of suffering may be the only way to survive. I know there have been times in my life that if the joy of the Lord were not my strength, it would

78

have felt impossible to make it or keep going. Joy begins with a focus, not a feeling. I have already mentioned that joy is not dependent on circumstances. Remember, we are to rejoice "always." As a Christ-follower, joy should characterize our lives, no matter what our situation. We are not rejoicing in our circumstances but in the Lord.

It's okay to rejoice in the blessings God has given us—and we should, but the focus of our joy should be in the Giver even more than the gifts. Let's face it; everything we have has an expiration date. It's nice to enjoy them while we have them, but they were never given to us to be the ultimate source of our joy. Someday, they will all be gone, and we are left just with the Creator of it all. To rejoice in the Lord means deciding to focus on and celebrate everything we have in Christ. We can praise Him in the good times and the bad.

None of what I just shared comes naturally. We must live it intentionally until it becomes a way of life. Rejoicing is like exercising a muscle. We have to decide to rejoice in the Lord continually. We must repeatedly celebrate what we have in Christ. Yes, because it is counterintuitive to be grateful in all things, we must exercise that muscle until difficulty no longer sucks the life out of us.

We must learn to continually rejoice in the Lord, celebrating what we have in Christ no matter what's going on in our lives.

Adversity exposes our selfishness (mainly through how we react to it), reveals our need for God, and enlarges our inward capacity for true happiness and love for

God. Adversity does its work in the same way as exercise grows muscle—by breaking it down first. No one wants to pray for brokenness, but it is through brokenness that we grow in our character and relationship to God, making a way for Him to use us for His good purpose. He will use whatever state we are in to transform our lives, especially when it involves adversity.

It's okay and normal to feel an internal struggle through this. The worst thing you can do, though, is to let that muscle atrophy because there is too much at stake. We must learn to continually rejoice in the Lord, celebrating what we have in Christ no matter what's going on in our lives. We have only one chance at life. I hate to see anyone waste it because of a lack of knowledge of what they could be experiencing and how they can influence future generations.

> *Choose to shift your focus from your trials to your treasure.*

Sometimes, the only thing hindering us from experiencing joy is a decision. It's not always that easy, but that's where it starts. Do whatever it takes to get your focus on Christ and all He has done for you. Choose to shift your focus from your trials to your treasure. How do we do that?

For me, it's listening to worship music and praising God for His many attributes, then reading some of the psalms, the teachings of Jesus, or studying some of Paul's encouraging letters. Not to minimize what you might be going through, I need to say that pain and disappointment cannot be avoided in this life. We all are going to experience it to some extent.

Don't get so focused on your difficulty though that you miss out on what's important. May I remind you, we live in a fallen world. Don't let a negative situation or person rob you of your joy, which ultimately gives you peace. Whatever that thing or person is that is pulling you down, it's not worth it! Who and what is most important after all? God has already prepared and provided all that is necessary to satisfy your soul—not just for eternity, but also for the here and now.

> Don't let a negative situation or person rob you of your joy, which ultimately gives you peace.

Just think of it, the same God who created the entire universe in all its glory and splendor, also created you and cares for everything about you, including your struggles. He is not unaware of your hardship, but He is available and desires to carry you through it.

What are you anxious about, and what is it about those things that make you anxious? That will tell you what your root fear is leading to your anxiety.

As you devote yourself to prayer over these adversities, you will experience peace. This is dependent prayer, a "Lord I need you" kind of prayer. Don't ever feel like God gets tired of hearing you pray even the same prayers over and over again. The way to trouble God is *not* to go to Him with your needs, desires, and concerns. Are you afraid He might disappoint you? Have you felt disappointed in the past, making you feel that way? I can guarantee that if you have been disappointed in God, you have

81

not understood His will. He wants you to bring all that to Him in prayer.

Don't let that push you away from Him. He can take it, and He wants you to be honest with Him. He already knows your feelings, thoughts, and desires. He wants us to pour out our heart to Him. Ultimately what He wants from us also is a worship, praise-filled prayer of surrender. This should remind you that our suffering is not the whole story.

This tells us that we are in the hands of a loving sovereign God who cares for us. He guarantees us that when we pray that way, He will respond with a stabilizing, sustaining, supernatural peace that surpasses all understanding in our hearts and minds. This peace is only found in Christ Jesus. The peace *of* God only comes when we have peace *with* God. Even though we know we don't deserve it, we can have that peace when we put out trust in the Good Shepherd.

I want to encourage you, my friend—or your friend—whoever it is that is suffering from depression, anxiety, or fear, as I have said earlier, our beloved Lord Jesus Christ will never leave you nor forsake you (Hebrews 13:5). He is our Maker and is with us always. He watches continually over us. Sir Winston Churchill once said, "If you are going through Hell, keep going..." If you are experiencing angst, a restlessness in your spirit, that is a product of underlying fear resulting from an estrangement from God that needs to be established or restored.

When your identity is in the One who created you, it changes your whole perspective on life.

I implore you, in the midst of your adversity, weariness, and disappointment, press on! Give it all to the Lord, laying it all at the foot of the cross. I pray that He will rewire your brain and heart and that the disenchantment will leave you. I pray

The peace of God only comes when we have peace with God.

that your mind and emotions are restored to the perfection in which they were originally created.

WHAT IS GOD'S ANTIDOTE TO ALL THESE OVERWHELMING EMOTIONS?

Remember the hope of your calling. As a Christ-follower, you are chosen, accepted by God. No matter what anyone says, you are adopted into the family of God. The same power that raised Jesus from the dead lives in you. God calls us sons and daughters. He wants us to see ourselves as dearly loved, chosen, valuable, and secure children of God.

Consider the magnitude of that calling. We are not called to a religion or duty but to a relationship—with the living God where we are seen as holy and blameless in His sight—not because of anything we did, but because of what Jesus did for us on the cross.

You may feel like your body is riddled with battle scars, but think of the scars that Jesus bore for us. When we get to see Him at the end of our life, we will see the scars in His hands, feet, and side. We will see the wounds left by the crown of thorns on his head and the ripped-up skin on His back from the flogging He received before His crucifixion.

There is nothing more senseless and unjust as the crucifixion of the Son of God. It was an evil act, committed by cruel and cowardly people. But what did God do with that? He used it to accomplish the salvation of the world. The event itself was terrible, but the outcome was more than good. It was incredible, beyond measure. God made right what was overwhelmingly, indefensibly, outrageous and wrong. The result? The world's redemption.

If something bad has happened to you, know that bad is bad and wrong is wrong, no matter what the outcome happens to be. God can cause so much good to come from a tragedy. Good coming from the tragedy does not make the tragedy itself good and right. It never has been and it never will. The outcome and an event is not quite the same thing. A good outcome does not excuse or justify a bad event. But redemption operates differently, because God can and often does use the worst events possible to work out His redemptive plan, as we can obviously and most clearly see in the story of Jesus.

God can bring good out of your pain like Jesus's scars resulted in our salvation if we have accepted His indescribable gift of the exchanged life. The lessons learned and the character formed through your suffering can be used for His glory.

We need not look at adversity as "good" in and of itself, but that God can work "good" out of it. Paul tells us in Romans 8:28,

"And we know that for those who love God all things work together for good, for those who are called according to his purpose." This is not saying that all things that happen to us are good, but that He can and does use adversity in our life for good purposes. There are reasons, sometimes unseen at least at the time, when He will use a bad situation for His good intentions. This is a promise for believers.

We have already stated what miraculous things can happen on the other side of adversity. It is up to us how we process the difficulties that affect our lives and if we are willing to grow from lessons offered through those experiences. Have you been open to receive the hidden gift within those struggles? No matter how strong we may think we are, there is no way we can overcome tragedies and rise victorious over it without God's help.

So, as we look at all of this, adversity while extremely difficult to navigate and is real, in and of itself, is not the root of our problem, It's ultimately our stubborn will, lack of faith, and rebellion against God. God can use adversity to enlarge our capacity to trust Him and reflect His image. What matters to Him is that we are responsive to Him right where we are. Adversity is an inescapable reality since we live in a "fallen" world. As we experience such, we must look to God for perspective, strength, and comfort, which under the best of circumstances is bound to afflict us in some form or another.

Not to minimize, dismiss, or ignore the severity of pain we feel in the face of adversity, we must remember that God is God, writing His redemptive story and we already know that He wins in the end, and all will be well. We need to remember that our emotions don't define reality, God does, and His reality is redemptive. We need not look at adversity as "good" in and of itself, but that God can work "good" out of it. He doesn't expect us to submit to the adversity itself, but to *Him* in our adversity.

You are called to a purpose. There is no one like you. You have a unique DNA, skills, talents, and gifts that God has purposed for you to use for His glory. He has a purpose only you can fulfill because there is no one else like you. We are to do good works that He has prepared and planned for us even before we were born.

We have a *general* purpose to love God and people. We have a *specific* purpose which, when we discover it, becomes our holy ambition. When you discover your unique purpose and you begin to give your life away, carrying out your specific call, He will use you to make a difference even if it is just what you think is a little corner of your world. You have no idea how God can and will use what He calls you to do. We just need to be obedient and do it. When that happens, the spirit of God causes you to experience the peace of God and there is nothing like it. The greatest joy you will ever experience is when God uses you to bring joy to others.

I don't know what you have found your identity in before now, but you can have your identity in Christ. If you are a Christ-follower, He is your identity. When your identity is in the One who created you, it changes your whole perspective on life. Your identity is in Christ, not these struggles that tend to pull you down and away from your first love. As we think about our legacy, we should consider: are our circumstances going to leave an imprint on us, or are we going to leave an imprint of faith and obedience on our circumstances?

If you have not experienced the saving grace of having all your sins washed away by the Author of peace, if you want the power of sin broken in your life, where you have a new master—Christ, providing you with the power to say "no" to sin and "yes" to righteousness, and you want the peace we are talking about, then you need to come to the Great Shepherd.

I have written a book titled *Where Will You Spend Eternity? Not Sure? There's Still Time,* where I spell out what a Christian is and is not. It explains how to experience the grace and glory of salvation and to secure your place in heaven. Right now, are you absolutely sure you will go to heaven when you die?

If not, you need to read this book. It's a quick read, like this one, and I walk you through what it takes to become a Christ-follower and secure your place in heaven. I then guide you through the "Next Steps" to help you understand how to go from there to experience the incredible, abundant life in Christ with the power over sin that you can experience right now.

We are not guaranteed tomorrow. Why wait for something as important as this? First, you want the assurance that your destiny is heaven. Then, as a byproduct of that, you will learn by submission to the Great Shepherd, how to overcome fears, anxieties, depression, whatever it is that has been robbing you from experiencing an abundant, victorious life, attained by resting in His comfort and care. The Great Shepherd loves you so much and wants you to rest in Him s meet all your needs.

If you are already a Christ-follower, I'm sure you have family or friends you would love to have join you in heaven. This book can be a great resource to introduce them to Christ. If you feel like you are limping around in your faith, the *"Next Steps"* portion of my book could be really beneficial for you as well. *Be sure to pick your copy on Amazon.com today. Just scan this QR code.*

If you are a Christ-follower and desire to get out of your spiritual rut and go deeper in your walk with Christ, I have written another book called, *Living the Life You Always Wanted – Experience Peace, Joy, Power and Perfect Love in Uncertain Times.* It will take your Christian walk to a whole new level. Just scan this QR code.

For Daily Inspirational Quotes, connect with me on your favorite social platform:

https://DebbySibert.com
https://twitter.com/debbysibert
https://www.linkedin.com/in/debsibert/
https://www.pinterest.com/debbysibert/
https://www.instagram.com/debbysibert/
https://www.facebook.com/DebbySibertAuthor

P.S. I mentioned earlier that praise and worship are a powerful way to shift our focus from our fears and disappointments, to the heart of God, opening up ourselves to learn and experience His purpose for us. When our desires shift off ourselves, to praise Him for Who He is and what He has done for us, and trust Him with our future, as well as our present, putting our trust in Him, we will experience the peace discussed in this booklet and open up opportunities to learn the plans He has for us.

If you go to https://tinyurl.com/GodsAttributes

Or scan the this **QR** code, you can download a YouTube playlist I made of some of my favorite worship songs that melt my heart and take me into His presence every morning as well as a list I compiled of the "Attributes of God" along with definitions and a scripture verse for each to help you put your focus on God.

I find that the worship music softens my heart and brings me to a point in my quiet-time that I want to praise God for some of His many attributes on this list. This helps to get my heart right as I start each day using the **ACTS** method I shared earlier. I know of no better way to experience the peace of God than to start you day this way. Every day can be a "do-over" day as you start fresh with **A**doration, **C**onfession, **T**hanksgiving and **S**upplication.

I haves also included on the next page a list of bible verses I compiled from the Crosswalk.com blog which is a great resource for daily inspiration and devotionals to help you start you day *with your focus on the Lord, His love for you and His provision. Keep these verses handy as a reminder that as a Christ-follower, we need not fear for He is with us and even in us to provide whatever we need in any and every circumstance to get us through* **anything.**

Have you found this publication to be helpful? If so, would you be willing to take a moment and leave a review? I know we all rely on those before downloading a book, even when it's free. Your review just might help someone else find some answers or at least some comfort and relief to help them experience some peace and calm in the midst of their storms. Go to <u>*https://tinyurl.com/Antidote-Review*</u>
Or use this **QR** code to get to the review *page.*

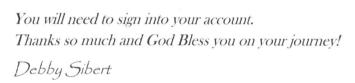

You will need to sign into your account.
Thanks so much and God Bless you on your journey!

Debby Sibert

PROMISES OF GOD

BIBLE VERSES TO REMIND US WE DO NOT HAVE TO FEAR:

Taken from New International Version (NIV)

1. "So do not fear, for I am with you; do not be dismayed, for I am your God. I will strengthen you and help you; I will uphold you with my righteous right hand." ~ Isaiah 41:10

2. "When I am afraid, I put my trust in you." ~ Psalm 56:3

3. "Do not be anxious about anything, but in every situation, by prayer and petition, with thanksgiving, present your requests to God. And the peace of God, which transcends all understanding, will guard your hearts and your minds in Christ Jesus." ~ Philippians 4:6-7

4. "Peace is what I leave with you; it is my own peace that I give you. I do not give it as the world does. Do not be worried and upset; do not be afraid." ~ John 14:27

5. "For God has not given us a spirit of fear, but of power and of love and of a sound mind." ~ 2 Timothy 1:7

6. "There is no fear in love. But perfect love drives out fear, because fear has to do with punishment. The one who fears is not made perfect in love." ~ 1 John 4:18

7. "When anxiety was great within me, your consolation brought joy to my soul." ~ Psalm 94:19

8. "But now, this is what the Lord says...Fear not, for I have redeemed you; I have summoned you by name; you are mine." ~ Isaiah 43:1

9. "An anxious heart weighs a man down, but a kind word cheers him up." ~ Proverbs 12:25

10. "Have I not commanded you? Be strong and courageous. Do not be terrified; do not be discouraged, for the Lord your God will be with you wherever you go." ~ Joshua 1:9

11. "Therefore do not worry about tomorrow, for tomorrow will worry about itself. Each day has enough trouble of its own." ~ Matthew 6:34

12. "Humble yourselves, then, under God's mighty hand, so that he will lift you up in his own good time. Leave all your worries with him, because he cares for you." ~ 1 Peter 5:6-7

13. "Tell everyone who is discouraged, Be strong and don't be afraid! God is coming to your rescue..." ~ Isaiah 35:4

14. "Do not worry about your life, what you will eat; or about your body, what you will wear. Life is more than food, and the body more than clothes. Consider the ravens: They do not sow or reap, they have no storeroom or barn; yet God feeds them. And how much more valuable you are than birds! Who of you by worrying can add a single hour to his life? Since you cannot do this very little thing, why do you worry about the rest?" ~ Luke 12:22-26

15. "The Lord is my light and my salvation—whom shall I fear? The Lord is the stronghold of my life—of whom shall I be afraid?" ~ Psalm 27:1

16. "Cast your cares on the Lord and he will sustain you; he will never let the righteous fall." ~ Psalm 55:22

17. "Immediately he spoke to them and said, 'Take courage! It is I. Don't be afraid.'" ~ Mark 6:50

18. "Be strong and courageous. Do not be afraid or terrified because of them, for the Lord your God goes with you; he will never leave you nor forsake you." ~ Deuteronomy 31:6

19. "'For I am the Lord, your God, who takes hold of your right hand and says to you, Do not fear; I will help you. Do not be afraid, for I myself will help you,' declares the Lord, your Redeemer, the Holy One of Israel." ~ Isaiah 41:13-14

20. "God is our refuge and strength, an ever-present help in trouble." ~ Psalm 46:1

21. "The Lord is with me; I will not be afraid. What can man do to me? The Lord is with me; he is my helper." ~ Psalm 118:6-7

22. "Fear of man will prove to be a snare, but whoever trusts in the Lord is kept safe." ~ Proverbs 29:25

23. "The angel of the Lord encamps around those who fear him, and he delivers them." Psalm 34:7

24. "But even if you suffer for doing what is right, God will reward you for it. So don't worry or be afraid of their threats." ~ 1 Peter 3:14

25. "I prayed to the Lord, and he answered me. He freed me from all my fears." ~ Psalm 34:4

26. "Do not be afraid of them; the Lord your God himself will fight for you." ~ Deuteronomy 3:22

27. "Then he placed his right hand on me and said: 'Do not be afraid. I am the First and the Last.'" ~ Revelation 1:17

28. "Jesus told him, 'Don't be afraid; just believe.'" ~ Mark 5:36

28. "And I am convinced that nothing can ever separate us from God's love. Neither death nor life, neither angels nor demons, neither our fears for today nor our worries about tomorrow—not even the powers of hell can separate us from God's love." ~ Romans 8:38-39

30. "The Lord your God is in your midst, A victorious warrior. He will exult over you with joy, He will be quiet in His love, He will rejoice over you with shouts of joy." ~ Zephaniah 3:17

31. "He who dwells in the shelter of the Most High will rest in the shadow of the Almighty. I will say of the Lord, "He is my refuge and my fortress, my God, in whom I trust."...He will cover you with his feathers, and under his wings you will find refuge; his faithfulness will be your shield and rampart. You will not fear the terror of night, nor the arrow that flies by day, nor the pestilence that stalks in the darkness, nor the plague that destroys at midday. A thousand may fall at your side, ten thousand at your right hand, but it will not come near you...For he will command his angels concerning you, to guard you in all your ways..."Because he loves me," says the Lord, "I will rescue him; I will protect him, for he acknowledges my name. He will call upon me, and I will answer

him; I will be with him in trouble, I will deliver him and honor him..." from Psalm 91:1-16

Be assured, He is with you in whatever you face, in the turmoil and struggles, amidst the anxious thoughts and the worries of life. He is there, strengthening, helping, and He holds you in His hands.

God is greater. He gives us the power to live courageously, boldly, fearlessly in this life, when many things that surround us would tell us to be afraid. His truth whispers strong and sure to the deepest core of our spirits.

"Do not fear."

All of that stuff on your mind? Give it to Him – again. Replace those fearful thoughts with His words of truth. And sleep in peace tonight. He knows what concerns you, He's got you covered.

Peace.[1]

1. https://www.crosswalk.com/blogs/debbie-mcdaniel/33-verses-to-remind-us--we-do-not-have-to-fear.html

Words of Encouragement:

Psalm 121

I lift up my eyes to the hills.
From where does my help come?
My help comes from the Lord,
who made heaven and earth.

He will not let your foot be moved;
He who keeps you will not slumber.
Behold, He who keeps Israel
will neither slumber nor sleep.

The Lord is your keeper;
the Lord is your shade on your right hand.
The sun shall not strike you by day,
nor the moon by night.

The Lord will keep you from all evil;
He will keep your life.
The Lord will keep
your going out and your coming in
from this time forth and forevermore.

THE SERENITY PRAYER
By Reinhold Niebuhr (1932)

This prayer has evolved into many forms over the years, the shorter most common and well known version:

God grant me the serenity to accept the things I cannot change,
Courage to change the things I can,
And wisdom to know the difference.

This is my favorite (original - full) version:

God, give me grace to accept with serenity
the things that cannot be changed,
Courage to change the things
which should be changed,
and the Wisdom to distinguish
the one from the other.

Living one day at a time,
Enjoying one moment at a time,
Accepting hardship as a pathway to peace,
Taking, as Jesus did,
This sinful world as it is,
Not as I would have it,
Trusting that You will make all things right,
If I surrender to Your will,
So that I may be reasonably happy in this life,
And supremely happy with You forever in the next.

Amen.

Where Will You Spend Eternity
Not Sure? There's Still Time

If you do not yet know Christ and the reason you must have a relationship with Him, then you need to read my first book, Where Will You Spend Eternity? If you are not sure whether or not you're going to heaven when you die, this book is for you.

We live in a busy world, don't we? Do you find yourself living just in the present? Do you ever think much about or plan for the future—not just retirement, but beyond the grave?

What is your destiny? What will happen to you when you die? Do you know for certain where you're headed, or are you not quite sure? Do you even know how serious that question is? The Bible tells us that once we die, our body decays, but our spirit lives on forever. If that's true, and it is, then it's essential to know where you will spend eternity.

That's what this book is all about. You can positively know you will go to heaven; but not everyone gets to go there. The alternative destination is catastrophic which you must avoid at all costs. It's essential to get that straightened out now while you're still alive and have the chance to change the trajectory of your life.

If you let them, the truths in this book can truly change your life for eternity.

If you are a Christ-follower, you can join many others who have found this to be a great ministry tool in sharing the gospel with those you love, care about and want to see in heaven! This is a short, quick read and when taken to heart, will change lives!

Grab your copy Right Now! Just go to Amazon.com and type in the title or scan this QR code:

Living the Life Your Always Wanted
Experience Peace, Joy, Power and Perfect Love During Uncertain Times.

Does the life you are experiencing right now line up with what you know to be what God offers through the Scriptures? Do you ever feel lethargic and distant from God? If you were to die today, would most people assume that you were going to heaven as they look at your lifestyle? What you seek is what you get. What are you seeking?

Do you lack peace or joy in your life—feeling stuck in your Christian walk? Do you find yourself wondering if there is more to the "abundant, victorious" life?

Too often, we settle for far less than what God wants to do in and through us. Do you sense that there may be more that God wants to do in and through you than you are currently experiencing?

The cornerstone of the extraordinarily victorious, transformed Christian life is a vital spiritual union with the risen Christ—available only through God's grace. When God created you, He created a masterpiece, and He has an exceptional plan and purpose for your life.

If you are not sure what that is, I hope to help you figure it out with the use of Scripture, referring to our "Life's Manual" (the

Bible) as the foundation of that discovery. My third book, *Living the Life You Always Wanted,* will help you to learn how to experience an amazing, abundant, victorious life of peace, joy, power and perfect love.

Do you want to take your life experience to the next level? If our answer is "yes" to any of these questions, then this book is for you.

Look it up on Amazon, or scan this QR code:

Choose Wisely
A 31 Day Devotional
Learn How to Make Choices to Transform Your Life

Have you found that some of the many choices you make on a daily basis have become habits that don't serve you well? We have to become intentional about avoiding those poor choices to experience a better way of life.

Do you want to make a positive impact and leave the world around you a bit better than you found it? Then let's choose to make wiser decisions remembering that words matter, character counts and our conduct—what we think, say and do reveals our heart.

The purpose of this 31-day devotional series is to help us all focus on godly characteristics and attributes that can become a daily part of our character and equip us to make wise choices.

When we make wise choices based on God's word, they will bring us the satisfaction in life that we all long for, which will gradually transform our lifestyle into one that will be an example for others and point them to Christ.

My goal in this series is to help you fall in love with Jesus in a new and fresh way as we discuss all these character qualities that He modeled for us in the Scriptures. As we focus our attention on His attributes and embrace an eternal perspective, imitating what he modeled for us, the more we will think and act like Him. Isn't that awesome? We become like those with whom we spend the most time.

The way we think affects how we feel, and how we feel affects the way we behave. If we want to change the way we act, we must go back and change our thoughts and choices.

We are only as close to God as we choose to be. Keep in mind, God gives us the freedom to make choices; however, we have to deal with, and don't get to choose the consequences of both the good and bad choices we make.

Jesus *chose* to die for us. The least we can do is to choose to live for Him.

Grab your copy Right Now! Just go to Amazon.com and type in the title or scan this QR code:

Forever is a Long Time to be Wrong
What is Your Destiny?

This book, *Forever Is a Long Time to Be Wrong*, is for those who struggle to believe there is a God or the Bible is true and relevant. In simple layman's terms, I help answer some hard questions, backed by thought-provoking evidence which I hope and pray will challenge any of your previously "preconceived" ideas about God, Creation, the resurrection, and the reliability of the Bible among other things.

Do you call yourself an atheist, agnostic, or a skeptic when it comes to God, Christianity, the reliability of the Bible, the validity of the resurrection, creation and all those Christian buzz words? Maybe you're a "none"—someone who doesn't want to be associated with any religious belief.

Could it be that perhaps you have bought into a lie that all the above is false? Could it be you have accepted your parents' beliefs without doing your due diligence to research the truth for yourself?

Could it be you made a religious decision when you were a child based on what you knew at the time and are stuck there not giving it much thought now that you are older and more mature?

One thing we both can agree on is someday we will die. I'm telling you there are only two destinations—heaven and hell, and we don't just return to dust.

If you don't believe that, forever is a long time to be wrong. Once you leave this world, there is no chance to change your mind. It will be too late. The time to get that figured out and straightened out is now while you are still alive.

If you did not want to have anything to do with God while on this earth, He will not force you to spend eternity with Him. He will say, "thy will be done" and you will be separated from Him or anything good forever.

The purpose of this book is to help walk you through some difficult questions with reliable evidence that hopefully will convince you of the need to make a U-turn. We are not promised tomorrow, and every breath we take is a gift. Please don't put this off!

God's Toolbox for a Fulfilling Marriage
Learn What the Required Tools Are and How to Acquire Them

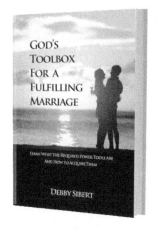

This book for couples, *God's Toolbox for Marriage,* is still in my head and my heart. I will get it in print as soon as I am able. My husband and I have been mentoring struggling married couples officially for over sixteen years, unofficially for decades. This is my passion because I know an amazing marriage is fully possible and am so sad that many couples never get to experience it, at least after the honeymoon period is over and reality sets in.

Any marriage help book is basically a toolbox of tips regarding how to get along with your spouse in the interest of having a successful marriage. Success looks different to different people, but it goes without saying and would be fair to conclude that we all want to be happy in our relationships.

A "Christian" marriage help book will go way beyond the typical psychology of "getting along." In this particular marriage manual, before the various tools for communication, conflict resolution, etc., are discussed, the content is focused on the foundational principles found in Scripture which teaches how to live lives of obedience and surrender to Christ which then gives us the ability to love and serve one another as Christ modeled.

There is no way we can have the ultimate marriage without having the guidance and direction of the Holy Spirit to empower us to love perfectly with the integrity and humility of Christ. It *IS* possible, and this book will give you the tools, encouragement, and instruction to achieve an amazing marriage that is the envy of all who know you.

Made in the USA
Las Vegas, NV
16 January 2022

41626003R00066